This book is for all of you who love old homes, old things and traditional design. I hope it inspires you to create beauty you love in your home too.

At Blackbird Cottage

Copyright © 2025 by Lindy Rahn

All rights reserved. This book or any portion thereof may not be reproduced or used in any manner whatsoever without the express written permission of the publisher except for the use of brief quotations in a book review.

Photography by Lindy Rahn.
Some images reprinted with kind permission of TradCo Architectural Hardware and Eliska Sharp.
Kitchen portrait and island shot by Eliska Sharp for County Style Magazine.
Mood board images reproduced with permission of owners.

Printed in Melbourne, Australia
First Printing, 2025
ISBN 978-1-7642853-0-8
Little Bird Books/Lindy Rahn
Cygnet, Tasmania, Australia

at BLACKBIRD COTTAGE

stories, style & the art of making a home

Lindy Rahn

CONTENTS

01 WHERE STORIES BEGIN
The beginnings of Blackbird Cottage Style — 5

02 HOW A HOUSE FINDS ITS VOICE
The elements that comprise Blackbird Cottage Style — 13

03 FINDING THE HEART OF A HOME
How rooms come alive — 55

04 THE COTTAGE THAT WAITED
A little house overlooked by the world, waiting for someone to notice her charm — 91

05 OUR STORY IN EVERY ROOM
The memories, meanings and little decisions that made this house our home — 111

06 WHERE THE GARDEN GROWS
Made from scratch and designed for beauty, utility and a little bit of wonder — 187

07 THE COTTAGE MADE BY HAND
Simple crafts and projects to bring beauty into the home — 199

WHERE STORIES BEGIN

A nostalgic heart, a lifelong love of old things, and
the journey that led to Blackbird Cottage

FIELD NOTES *No 1*

Discovered May 17 2023

OFFICE DOORFRAME | ORIGINAL
WALLPAPER & BORDER
MAYBE THE PARLOUR ROOM?

Tucked beneath layers of more modern wallpaper, this vivid floral border was pasted around the door. Perhaps once a bold choice for a formal front room.

WHERE STORIES BEGIN

A nostalgic heart, a lifelong love of old things, and the journey that led to Blackbird Cottage

Have you ever heard the phrase "an old soul"? I'm not sure if anyone has ever described me that way, but I can tell you there have been many times I've felt born in the wrong era—or, if I believed in reincarnation, that I've been here before.

For as long as I can remember, I've loved old houses. The details in their design, chimneys jutting into the sky, the charm of a small-paned window, all of it draws me in. I find their history irresistible. Old houses tell the story of those who built them and the families who lived there through generations. Each home holds a time capsule, treasures waiting to be discovered. And over the years, we've uncovered more than a few.

"As a girl, I longed for history in every room—a creak in the floorboards, a threadbare chair, a story waiting to be uncovered."

When I was a little girl, my school holiday wish list always included a trip to our local museum to admire the displays of historical paraphernalia. I adored the grim-faced mannequins in 19th-century garb, cracked porcelain, and furniture far too small for any modern-day bottom. I'm fairly certain the rest of my family didn't share my fascination, but I could wander for hours through heritage houses, marvelling at cedar banisters and hidden servant staircases. I spent countless afternoons in the historical section of our local library, poring over artefacts.

I loved imagining myself dressed in 'olden day' clothes—an empire-line gown, ringlets in my hair, and satin slippers on my feet. I seized any chance to dress the part. At around age eleven, I made a hoop to wear under a dress. I have no idea why, though it was probably the same year I devoured *The Secret Garden* and *Little House on the Prairie*.

As I grew older, I fell in love with hand-stitched clothing and ruffled shirts, though I never dared tell my disco-loving friends. They would have laughed. While they watched *Grease* and *Saturday Night Fever*, I daydreamed of windswept moors and sandstone cottages straight out of Thomas Hardy, or sitting at a writing desk like Jane Austen. I wanted to live in the world of the *Little Women*.

The time came when I wanted to move on from my ballerina-themed bedroom. I saved my pocket money and bought a roll-top desk and a vintage tea trolley. They were my first antique purchases. One served as a bedside table. Eventually, my grandmother gifted me her antique bedroom suite. The wardrobe didn't suit modern coat hangers, but I adored it. I kept that set for twenty-five years, even loaning it to my brother on the promise that if my daughter ever wanted it, he'd return it. I won't tell you what happened to that bedroom suite, but it made me sad.

My interior decorating style evolved over the years, and more than once I considered formal study and a new career. Starting a business where I could spend my days surrounded by fabric and wallpaper swatches sounded like heaven. But with a full-time teaching job, two children, and a husband who worked away from home two weeks out of every three, it wasn't practical. So, I dabbled. I experimented. My first attempts were… not great. Garish, if I'm honest. But then, my first time on roller skates wasn't great either.

For me, decorating is a skill, not instinct. You may be blessed with an eye for design but you also learn and refine it over time. I've made plenty of mistakes, and I still do. Things don't always look the way I picture them. It often takes a few furniture shuffles and a lot of shelf tweaking before I'm happy. Isn't that part of the fun? Or should I say the frustration?

Over the past three decades, the homes we lived in—and the seasons of life we were in—shaped me. Even when we built a glass-fronted, solar-passive house, I still found a place for a vintage dresser to display china. I refused to part with certain pieces.

If something didn't quite fit the new home, I adapted it. That's how my style became what it is now: eclectic, layered, a blend of the secondhand and the new. I've pored over magazines and repainted the same walls more times than I care to admit. But, eventually, a style emerged that's distinctly my own. It's the style that sets my heart alight. It wasn't until this home that it received a name: Blackbird Cottage Style.

Within the pages of this book, you'll find my journey as a decorator and how it took shape within the walls of Blackbird Cottage. You'll discover the elements that make up Blackbird Cottage Style, my creative process, and how the renovation shaped each room's evolution. Think of it as a journal you've been invited to step into, a glimpse inside the way I think, the way I dream.

I hope it inspires you to begin something of your own.

Lindy xoxo

THE HOMES THAT SHAPED MY STYLE
a visual timeline of the spaces we called home

Our First Home

The Dollhouse

OUR FIRST HOME
Little Pink Cottage
1987

The Bush House
1992

The Dollhouse
1996

The Colourful House
2002

The Glasshouse
2011

Green Gate Farm

The Convict House

EVERY HOME A CHAPTER,
every design a step closer to Blackbird Cottage Style

The Terrace House

The Colourful House

The Terrace Cottage — 2015

The Convict House — 2016

Green Gate Farm — 2018

Blackbird Cottage — 2023

The Glasshouse

Blackbird Cottage
OUR STORY CONTINUES...

02

HOW A HOUSE FINDS ITS VOICE

From mismatched walls to meaningful layers.
A journey toward Blackbird Cottage Style.

FIELD NOTES No 2

Purchased March 1987

PROUD NEW HOMEOWNERS | OBLIVIOUS AS TO WHAT'S TO COME

We barely knew one end of a paintrush from the other, and somehow convinced a bank to give us a mortgage. The house? A 1940s weatherboard with loads of... rats.

HOW A HOUSE FINDS ITS VOICE

From mismatched walls to meaningful layers—how Blackbird Cottage Style began.

A long time ago, a young couple fell in love and decided to settle down together. They had no money for a house deposit, so the guy sold his beloved MG and put the cash aside. Excited, they circled possibilities in the newspaper and went house hunting, even though they had to stick to a tight budget.

The couple's options in good neighbourhoods were limited, but at last they found a place within reach. The day they went to view it they saw other potential buyers leaving the Open Home gagging—literally. The house was that disgusting. It wasn't layout, dampness or structural issues that sent people running, because none of those were present. It was the stench inside, a kitchen so dated and useless it seemed an expensive fix, a bathroom that hadn't been cleaned for years, and stained, rotten curtains. But the couple saw the house with different eyes. Despite its flaws, the house simply needed love, a factor missing for a long time. So, with a guiding parent by their side, reassuring them it was "a good buy," they took the plunge and purchased the little house.

That couple was us, and that house was our first home: a two-bedroom 1940s timber cottage with crusted vomit up the walls, layers of rugs hiding dog mess, a massive flea infestation that took three exterminator visits to clear, and rats. Yes, rats. It was filthy and revolting, and our friends thought we were insane. But we had a vision. We've always had vision. I loved that house. It was ours, and we could do whatever we wanted.

Within days of settlement, Gavin and I rolled up our sleeves and, with my dad pitching in, we built simple cabinetry for the kitchen, because the only thing we had was a sink and two overhead cupboards. I found a white-and-blue polka dot wallpaper for above the dado rail, which I painted navy. We spray-painted the 1950s fridge to match and laid cork flooring. My first kitchen hutch stood against the wall, and I began collecting blue and white china with help from one of my grandmothers. A pine kitchen table and a set of directors' chairs claimed the middle of the room, and a blue gingham café curtain framed the lone window, shielding the view of our neighbour's house. That was where good taste came to an end.

Inspired by magazine clippings I'd saved, I tackled our hallway, painting it a sunny yellow with lilac trim. It was light filled and gorgeous, perfect for a modern '80s home, but for our quaint little cottage? Not so much. Especially when the kitchen was navy blue and white. The real design disaster struck in the bedroom, where I hung salmon wallpaper adorned with dainty white flowers and painted white trim on the windows and door. It was perfection, until you saw it next to that yellow. A mismatch, plain and simple.

Years later, I stumbled across the same fabric and textile collection at a shop holding a closing down sale and, feeling nostalgic, I bought some. I made the fabric into pillows which I use in Blackbird Cottage today. Why? Because that was a timeless pattern. I just had no clue how to use it.

> *"I knew nothing about sightlines, or how colours in one room should harmonise with those in another."*

I didn't realise how outdoor light could alter the tone of interior paint. I didn't know about mixing colours and patterns. I copied styles and pictures without any understanding of what I was doing or why. Sometimes it worked, sometimes it didn't. But I gave it a go.

I hung cabbage rose-patterned Austrian blinds in the living room—blinds that had no business being in the same space as the gold velvet hand-me-down sofa or the Persian-style rug. I wanted those blinds because other people had them.

This cottage in Devon was built in the 1300s. I've always noticed details, and the carving on the newel post, tucked into a sweet cottage setting, caught my eye. It made me wonder who else had walked those stairs and what the origin of the house was.

Our baby's room was a mix of pale blue and cream, with cross-stitch craft on the wall, hand-sewn quilts on the bed and antique furniture. His first bed was a cabin bed with drawers underneath, which we found in a second-hand shop and painted cream to match his decor. The sunroom, with its deep olive walls, sandy trims and seagrass flooring, had no purpose at all. It sat empty.

Individually, each room had charm. But together? Let's just say it was chaos.

Within three years, I realised my mistakes. Out went the mismatched colours, replaced with something more cohesive that let us walk through our home without getting a migraine from the sensory overload. The living spaces turned a shade of dusky rose that blended with our carpet and the wallpaper. The kitchen stayed blue, but I added pink accents to tie it together. I'd learned a valuable lesson, one I never forgot.

Still, I'm grateful for that young woman who, armed with paint cans and a stack of *Better Homes and Gardens* magazines, tackled it with such enthusiasm. She learned to be fearless as a decorator, to explore her creative side and stay resourceful, honing skills that shaped the Blackbird Cottage Style I love today. Because of her experiments, I learned to plan and consider, to mix new with old and, at the end of the day, to remember "it's only paint."

My style has matured since then, yet it's always embraced cottage, vintage, repurposed pieces and a love of colour. And now, "cottage style" is back in vogue, not that I care, because I've never followed trends.

When someone asks me to define my style, I say, "English Cottage." Yet my style isn't the overly chintzy, overstuffed look. It's more pared back, and while keeping the English Cottage elements of curation and layering, it remains utterly personal to us. Decorating labels can box you in, and I find more joy in eclectic collections. That's why my home feels like a tapestry of influences, where a Victorian oak chest of drawers lives comfortably next to an IKEA sofa, and cedar colonial pieces mingle with pine cottage antiques.

When I imagine my style, I see a welcoming entry with ever-changing decor, a pair of topiaries one week, a twig wreath the next. The entry draws you into a colourful, patterned interior that feels balanced, not overwhelming, and filled with art, rugs and cherished collections.

Blackbird Cottage Style isn't about clutter; it's about intention. It's layered but not overloaded, cosy without sacrificing function. It doesn't look like a furniture showroom. It's old and well-loved but it's not a dusty antique shop or my great grandmother's living room.

Dusting isn't a priority, so knickknacks are kept to a minimum, and every piece is chosen thoughtfully, not for trend but for heart. Yes, trend items may appear but they've been selected for their ability to fit the aesthetic of my home, not because they're fashionable.

Too many samples to count

Fabrics collected and stored for use somewhere

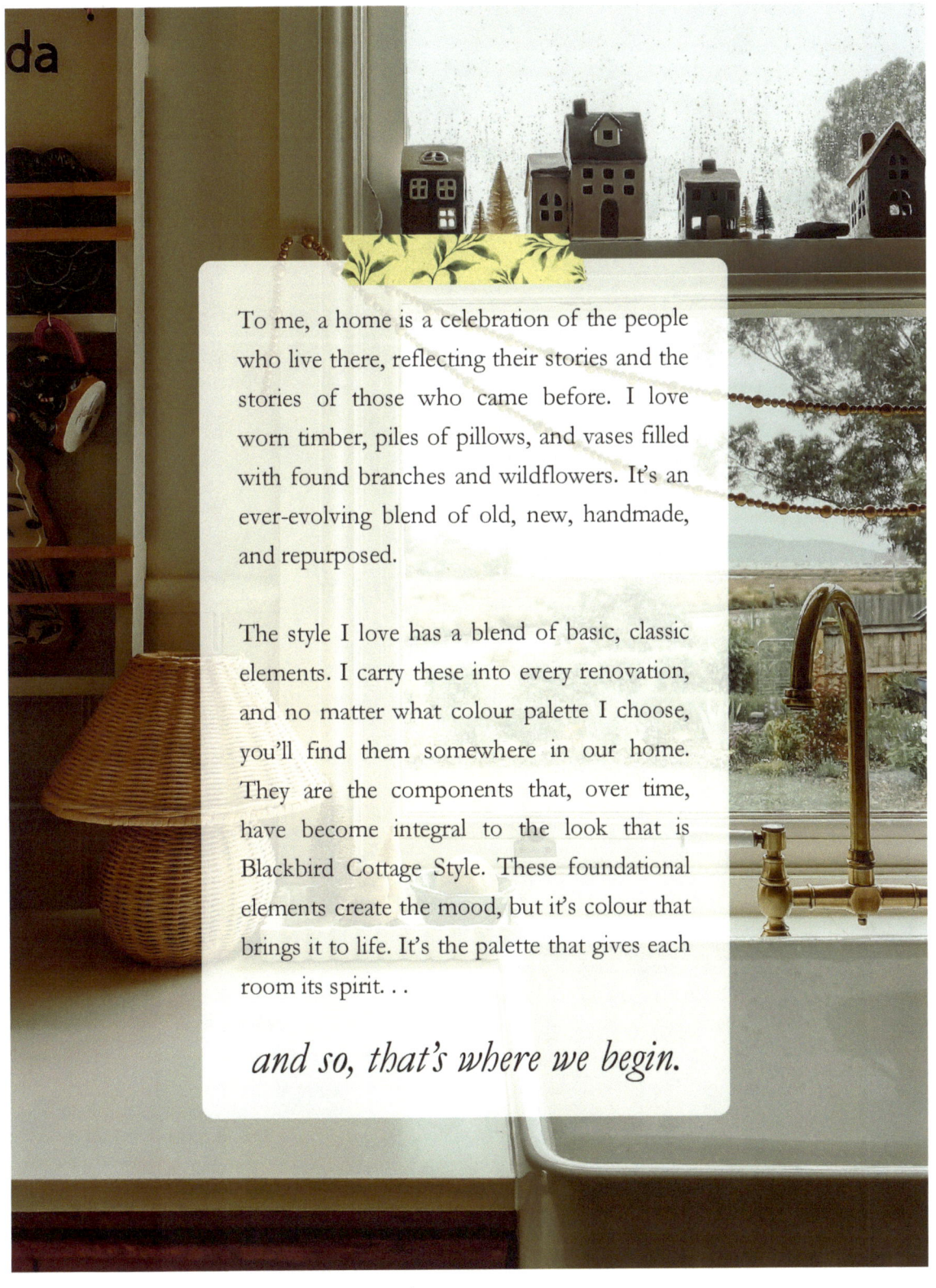

To me, a home is a celebration of the people who live there, reflecting their stories and the stories of those who came before. I love worn timber, piles of pillows, and vases filled with found branches and wildflowers. It's an ever-evolving blend of old, new, handmade, and repurposed.

The style I love has a blend of basic, classic elements. I carry these into every renovation, and no matter what colour palette I choose, you'll find them somewhere in our home. They are the components that, over time, have become integral to the look that is Blackbird Cottage Style. These foundational elements create the mood, but it's colour that brings it to life. It's the palette that gives each room its spirit. . .

and so, that's where we begin.

QUICK TIP
TO CREATE COHESION WITH COLOUR

Choose one colour you love, then repeat it in different shades and materials throughout the room. It brings harmony without feeling matchy-matchy.

THE HEAD GARDENER'S COTTAGE
Birmhingham Botanical Gardens

THE LANGUAGE OF COLOUR

CHEERY EXTERIOR YELLOW |
NO PERMISSION SLIPS FROM THE
NEIGHBOURS WERE SIGNED

Whenever we move to a new home, and we've done that a lot, I feel an immediate surge of excitement about the space and the endless possibilities for creativity. From the moment we sign the contract, I mentally start designing the interior, imagining how to make the house feel like ours. Even if no major renovations are needed, I feel compelled to put my stamp on it, to feather my nest. A house doesn't feel like home until the boxes are unpacked and I've left my mark. Even rental homes need a bit of "me" in them before my inner self can relax. For me, the process of making a home usually means adding colour and surrounding myself with my things. If those elements are missing, there's always a price to pay, and it's not a harmless one. My mental health suffers if I'm not in a space I truly enjoy.

Back in the early 2000's, we moved 3,000 kilometres from Tasmania to Western Australia. We rented a townhouse for a year: central to the city and close to my teaching job, which was essential since Gavin was working away and I was basically a single parent for two weeks in three. It was also one of the few furnished houses in a decent neighbourhood.

LITTLE KEEPSAKE *No 1*
A paint swatch, sunshine yellow, found stuffed in my pocket after a hardware shop visit. Colour has the power to change the character of an exterior.

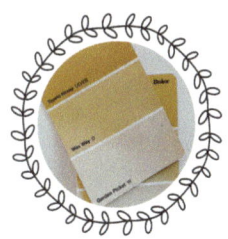

The plan was to test out the WA lifestyle before committing, so we took only our clothing and personal items on the journey with us. We promised the children that, after a year, we'd take a family vote on whether to stay or return to Tasmania. (And I think, secretly, I was hoping they'd want to go back. Moving across the country was not something I really wanted to do.)

The townhouse itself was perfectly okay. The rooms were generous, there were two bathrooms and it had great views of the ocean. The interior colour palette, on the other hand, left a lot to be desired. It was monotone. The owners had clearly gone down the route of 'buy in bulk and paint everything to match'. There were grey walls, grey cabinetry, grey tiles, grey carpet, grey curtains and yes, grey furniture. To make matters worse, it wasn't even an interesting grey; it was the same shade of cold, lifeless office grey that would work fine in a workspace where you're only in the room for a few hours at a time. For a home? It was soul sucking. If Eeyore were a townhouse, that house was it. And the house was sad.

I lasted a year in that house. It didn't feel like home for a single second, and I was miserable the entire time we lived there. During that year, I developed an aversion to pale grey that borders on psychosis inducing, and a realisation that I am not a 'neutral' person. Not even in my Farmhouse era could I have been termed neutral, and believe me, I tried.

When we finally moved into our own home, I let loose with colour. The entry hall in the new house, once a nice, calm beige was bathed in pumpkin. Chocolate and avocado green appeared on feature walls. The dining room housed a berry red hutch stacked with my blue china. And while it might sound like I was decorating for a foodie phase, the colours suited the house beautifully. It worked. And the reason it worked? The colours in each space were tempered with crisp, neutral whites on the majority of the walls and the rooms were filled with modern furniture. The walls became a vibrant backdrop for our growing art collection, and when tied in with a mix of vintage pieces, it felt like home. So at home, we sold the Tassie house, shipped our belongings to WA and stayed eight years in that house.

an emerald floor

a berry red hutch

a rosy door

In the years that followed, we completed a major renovation. We upgraded from the cheap builder fittings to more custom ones, adding a pool and creating an outdoor living area to use every day. Our children spent their teen years there and many happy memories were created. It was the longest period of time we ever spent in one place. And it wasn't an old house, it was a house filled with colour and we felt very settled. However, as with all our homes, I learned a decorating lesson I will never forget. The brave foray into technicolour taught me, **paint first, regret later.**

Trying to match sofas, curtains, and accessories to a previously chosen paint colour is the design equivalent of doing a puzzle with missing pieces. Our home looked pretty, but it lacked layers and depth. I could never find the accessories I was looking for in a colour that coordinated with the paint colours. I'd gone about decorating the wrong way and wasted time and money in the process. If I had chosen my textiles first, or based the scheme on a hero piece in my rooms, I could have matched paint to that. I thought picking a colour created the scheme and the rest was easy. (Spoiler: it wasn't). It turned out there was a sequence to successful decorating, and it had been sheer luck that I'd managed to create homes we loved before. Twenty years on, I've come full circle. I know I must have colour. Muted or bright, it makes us happy in our home. I am not afraid to slap paint on a wall because, I know the steps to follow to make that colour work in the room. I've also devised a system for creating a scheme, one that helps me choose the right colour (most of the time!) but more on that later.

QUICK TIP
TO COMBINE PATTERNS EFFORTLESSY

Choose a solid, a check and a print in similar tones. Mixing textures adds interest without overwhelming the space

THE POETRY OF PATTERN

WILLIAM MORRIS LIVES AGAIN | MY OFFICE, 2023

The use of pattern, whether in decor, soft furnishings, bedding, or wallpaper, is a cornerstone of Blackbird Cottage Style.

The day wallpaper came back into fashion was a happy one. Before that, I relied on fabric and textiles to bring pattern into the home. I layered bed linens, sofa cushions, table runners, and curtains. I refreshed vintage chairs with new upholstery, and made pillows to adorn the bed. Wherever possible, I wove pattern into a space, using it to create warmth and character. For me, pattern has always been the way to achieve cosy without tipping into clutter.

Wallpaper is not only found on walls in the cottage. I use wallpaper remnants to cover storage boxes and line the backs of cabinets with easily removable peel-and-stick paper. I've even used offcuts to create Christmas bows and decorations. Wallpaper acts as a patterned backdrop for other motifs in a room. I'm especially drawn to simple, classic prints such as small florals, delicate geometrics, and timeless stripes in colours that feel rooted in tradition. These designs sit comfortably with vintage furniture and collected pieces.

LITTLE KEEPSAKE *No 2*
A scrap of gingham left from making cushion covers. Pattern can turn the plainest corner into something soft and welcoming.

Wallpaper often inspires my accent colours but can stand alone as a decorative feature, allowing me to leave walls unadorned and let the wallpaper be the hero. There's no need to fill my walls with a gallery of art when the walls themselves tell the story.

Mixing patterns such as gingham, stripes, and petite geometric prints is another of my favourite ways to bring pattern into our home.

Gingham is a key design element at Blackbird Cottage, covering the bed linens, tablecloths, and pillow covers. I prefer the classic size with squares around a centimetre in width. It's just the right balance: small enough to feel traditional but large enough to show off the pattern. Too tiny, and it might as well be a solid; too big, and it ventures into gaudy territory. Gingham is the perfect blend of casual and elegant, depending on the way it's used. As upholstery on a chair it can add an air of playful elegance, but as a table napkin it has a romantic, yet casual feel.

Florals, botanicals and block prints are essential to the look. I favour smaller, cottage-style florals rather than the larger, more dramatic designs that, to me, can feel somewhat chintzy or outdated.

Pattern on pattern is a commitment, not a flirtation

MINI FEATURE No 1

WHERE PATTERN BELONGS
Where pattern leaves it mark

- Curtains
- Lampshades
- Cushions
- Bed Linen
- China
- Painted on furniture
- Upholstery
- Rugs
- Wallpaper
- Accessories

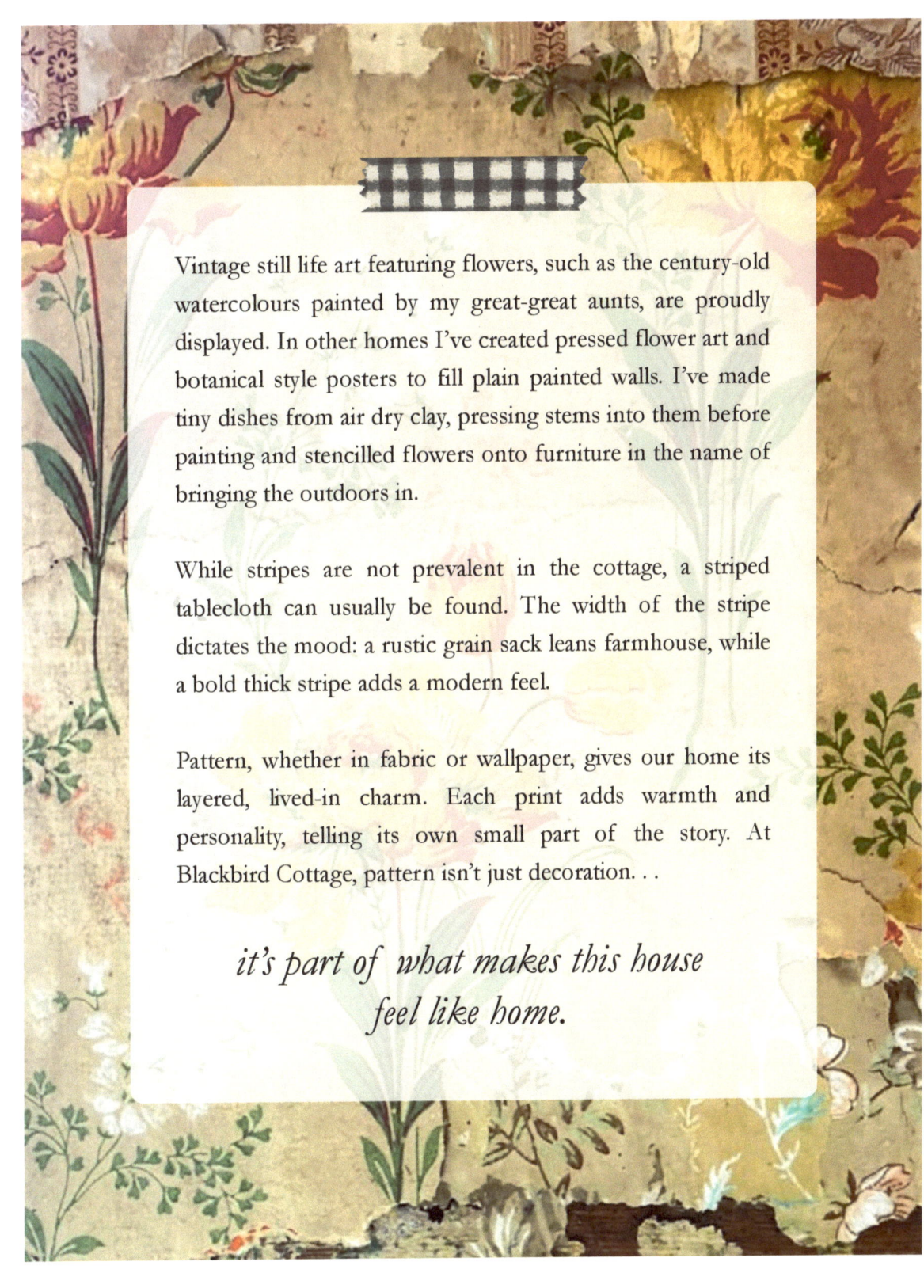

Vintage still life art featuring flowers, such as the century-old watercolours painted by my great-great aunts, are proudly displayed. In other homes I've created pressed flower art and botanical style posters to fill plain painted walls. I've made tiny dishes from air dry clay, pressing stems into them before painting and stencilled flowers onto furniture in the name of bringing the outdoors in.

While stripes are not prevalent in the cottage, a striped tablecloth can usually be found. The width of the stripe dictates the mood: a rustic grain sack leans farmhouse, while a bold thick stripe adds a modern feel.

Pattern, whether in fabric or wallpaper, gives our home its layered, lived-in charm. Each print adds warmth and personality, telling its own small part of the story. At Blackbird Cottage, pattern isn't just decoration. . .

it's part of what makes this house feel like home.

Patterns weave warmth into every corner, making the cottage feel both elegant and lived-in.

PATTERNS FOR A COTTAGE LOOK

The cottage in 2023 had too many layers of wallpaper to count, each one a piece of the cottage's history. This discovery reinforced my belief that, once we'd plastered, we should hang new wallpaper and honour the tradition, making the cottage feel as it once was, but with a twenty-first century twist. The new iteration of Blackbird Cottage features wallpapers by Boråstapeter and Morris & Co., brands that fit the aesthetic. They add a touch of old world charm, creating cosy yet elevated bedrooms, and a wow moment in the bathroom. Each wallpaper was chosen not only for its cottage appeal but as a nod to the heritage of the home. Below are other prints I love to use to create that cottage vibe.

Favourite Cottage Prints

Toile · Ticking · Florals
Block Print · Gingham · Tartan

QUICK TIP
TO STYLE WICKER AND RATTAN

Layer natural textures for warmth and charm. Mix wicker chairs with rattan trays or baskets to create depth without making the space feel heavy.

THE BEAUTY OF WOVEN THINGS

A RUG AND A BASKET | CLASSIC COSY TEXTURES

Baskets, chairs, trunks, and light fittings made from rattan, wicker, or cane bring a depth of texture and timeless charm to a home that cannot be overstated. The patina of vintage wicker, whether painted or left in its natural state, draws me in every time. Its ability to evoke a sense of nostalgia makes it hard for me to ignore. Wicker and rattan feel both rustic and refined. They effortlessly bridge the gap between casual comfort and elegance no matter where I use them in the cottage. The kind of rattan and wicker I favour is not trendy, boho-inspired or 70s in style. While I do love a wicker chest of drawers, my style leans toward vintage often with a little wear and tear. Picture a wicker chair nestled in the corner of the verandah, inviting long, lazy evenings, or a chunky woven basket next to the sofa, brimming with blankets. At Blackbird Cottage, wicker and rattan are elements that create harmony throughout the home. Scalloped rattan pendants add a whimsical touch to the bedrooms, while a custom oversized fixture in the kitchen defines the eating nook and provides a soft, dappled glow to the table area. In the main bedroom, I've used rattan shades on the wall sconces to bring texture and warmth.

LITTLE KEEPSAKE No 3
*A tartan throw brought home from a trip to Scotland—
a reminder of our cultural roots. Objects can tell the
story of a life and its journey.*

The chandelier in the lounge echoes the same idea, with a set of little woven shades softening the black wire and creating a moment of nubby texture against the board and batten ceiling.

The dogs each have a wicker basket, an extravagance that not only elevates the look of our living area, but allows Bonnie and Winnie to chill in style. In my office, a vintage wicker picnic basket sits inside a disused fireplace, discreetly storing documents, while a collection of newer baskets and boxes hide practical items on the bookshelf.

Natural textures, such as jute, pair beautifully with wicker at the cottage, bringing an organic quality to our rooms and a warmth and softness to otherwise cold floors. Blackbird Cottage features two jute rugs. A scalloped design has recently moved from the lounge to my office creating a playful tone against the traditional wallpaper, while a chunky navy rug in the guest bedroom adds a warm landing for feet on cold mornings.

These types of natural elements are budget friendly, and relaxed in style. They add warmth, texture, and cohesion to a home, while offering a connection to the handmade past and proving that practical pieces can also be beautiful.

A rattan lamp. Perfect for dark mornings

MINI FEATURE No 2

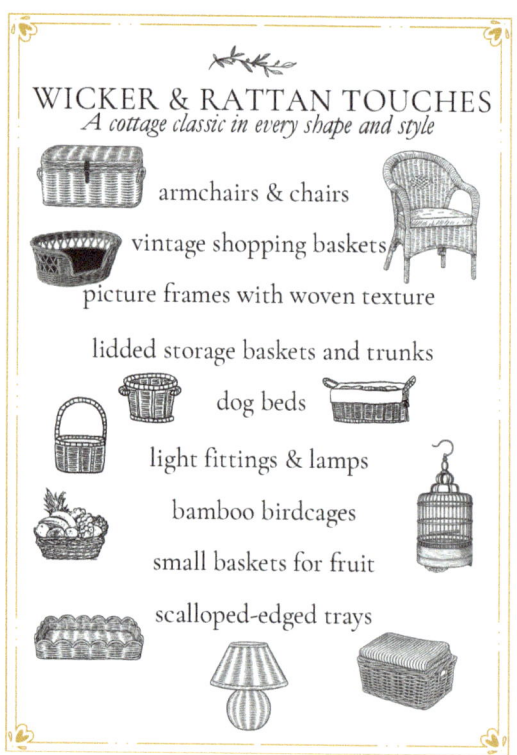

WICKER & RATTAN TOUCHES
A cottage classic in every shape and style

armchairs & chairs
vintage shopping baskets
picture frames with woven texture
lidded storage baskets and trunks
dog beds
light fittings & lamps
bamboo birdcages
small baskets for fruit
scalloped-edged trays

An old wicker chair, found for $15 at a scout sale, and now quite convinced its always lived in my office. It creaks just enough to be endearing and tucks perfectly into a corner or at the dining table for extra guest seating.

QUICK TIP
FOR CHARMING TABLE SETTINGS

Mix vintage china patterns for a collected look. A shared colour or motif will tie them together and keep the setting from feeling mismatched.

A LOVE OF LINEN AND CHINA

COLLECTED OVER DECADES | USED WITHOUT CEREMONY

If I had my way, I'd own every piece of stemware known to man, every floral dinner set, and all the napkin rings and linen napkins. But that would require a much larger house than our cottage, so I make do with what I have.

Pretty tableware is simply an extension of how I like to show hospitality. Blackbird Cottage Style means a table set with a cloth, real napkins, not paper, and wine glasses. More often than not, I'll buy a length of linen or cotton fabric and sew simple hems to make a last minute tablecloth, it's much cheaper. I also keep a small stash of preloved tablecloths and china for special occasions.

The pricier linens in our house don't stay in a drawer. Blackbird Cottage Style is about curating a collection… and then using it. It's not about living in a display home or having "good china." My grandma didn't gift me her very expensive dinner set for it to gather dust. Yes, I've broken a few cups over the years, but I know she'd appreciate that I love and use her tableware. (And she'd giggle knowing I freak out our friends when I tell them how much the plates they're eating off are worth.)

LITTLE KEEPSAKE No 4
A single linen napkin, found at an op-shop for a dollar. A table can feel special, even when nothing quite matches.

Mixing old and new china brings an easy charm to the table. A stack of plain white plates can happily sit beside floral teacups, vintage platters, and mismatched bowls. The contrast adds warmth and makes every meal feel a little more special.

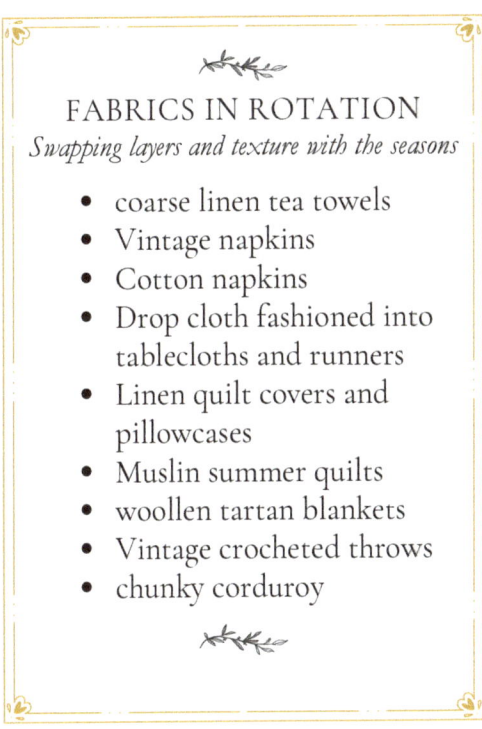

MINI FEATURE No 3

FABRICS IN ROTATION
Swapping layers and texture with the seasons

- coarse linen tea towels
- Vintage napkins
- Cotton napkins
- Drop cloth fashioned into tablecloths and runners
- Linen quilt covers and pillowcases
- Muslin summer quilts
- woollen tartan blankets
- Vintage crocheted throws
- chunky corduroy

China and stemware don't have to cost a fortune and can be mixed in to elevate a table setting. I own three dinner sets, plus a collection of vintage and seasonal plates, along with a few cheap knock-offs. I mix these to create new looks, adding different napkins or flatware to suit. One thing I do buy new is glassware. I find it hard to source second-hand sets, and I like my glasses to match. The same goes for flatware. My three sets are new, enough for a dozen people, but each with a different look: gold, chrome, and faux bamboo.

Natural textiles have become important to me over the years. As I grew older, I discovered my body doesn't react well to synthetic fabrics, so I've been gradually swapping these for natural fibres like wool, cotton or linen. Curating a look like this can be expensive, and the choices where we live are limited. But, I've learned to respect that, and now shop carefully for textiles, grabbing samples to check for quality and to ensure they suit the mood I want to create, giving off a more traditional feel.

caring for linen

Linen softens and improves with washing, and I've found it rewards a gentle hand. Over years of experimenting, I've discovered I get the best results when I wash our linen in cool water, using a mild detergent, and avoiding bleach which can weaken the fibres. A soft feel to the linen is achieved by spin drying on a low setting, or drying outdoors. By doing this I often don't need to iron. But, if you prefer a crisp look, iron while the linen is slightly damp, using a medium-hot setting. Store your linen in a cool, dry place, away from direct sunlight, and never in plastic because it needs to breathe.

QUICK TIP
FOR EASY FORAGING
Keep a pair of secateurs and a canvas tote in your car. You'll always be ready to snip wild blooms or branches when you chance upon them.

GIFTED, FORAGED & FOUND

COLLECTED FROM THE ROADSIDE | IT'S NOT STEALING, ITS COMMUNITY SERVICE

Seasonal foraging plays a part in bringing the outdoors into the cottage, and to me, there's nothing more beautiful than apple tree branches cut and woven into rustic wreaths, or dried flower heads displayed in a pitcher. Gathered roadside bulrushes, blossom, and crabapple branches create moments of seasonal charm on side tables or in large vases around our home, and they're a more sustainable way to decorate through the seasons.

Last spring, I found a branch in bud while taking our dog, Bonnie, for her daily swim. It was almost a metre tall and quite wide, which made for an interesting time fitting it into the back seat of the car, but I got it home. I 'planted' the branch in an oversized glass vase and arranged it on the cabinet next to the fireplace. Over the course of a couple of weeks, I changed the water and we watched as the buds opened into leaves and the branch bloomed fully. The spring season was coming to life in our living room. Then, as the Christmas season approached, I took the branch out to the backyard and added it to our compost heap. This kind of decorating is free, unique to you, and can never be replicated.

LITTLE KEEPSAKE No 5
A kangaroo paw collected from a neighbour. After months in a vase, it's dried to a perfect linen shade

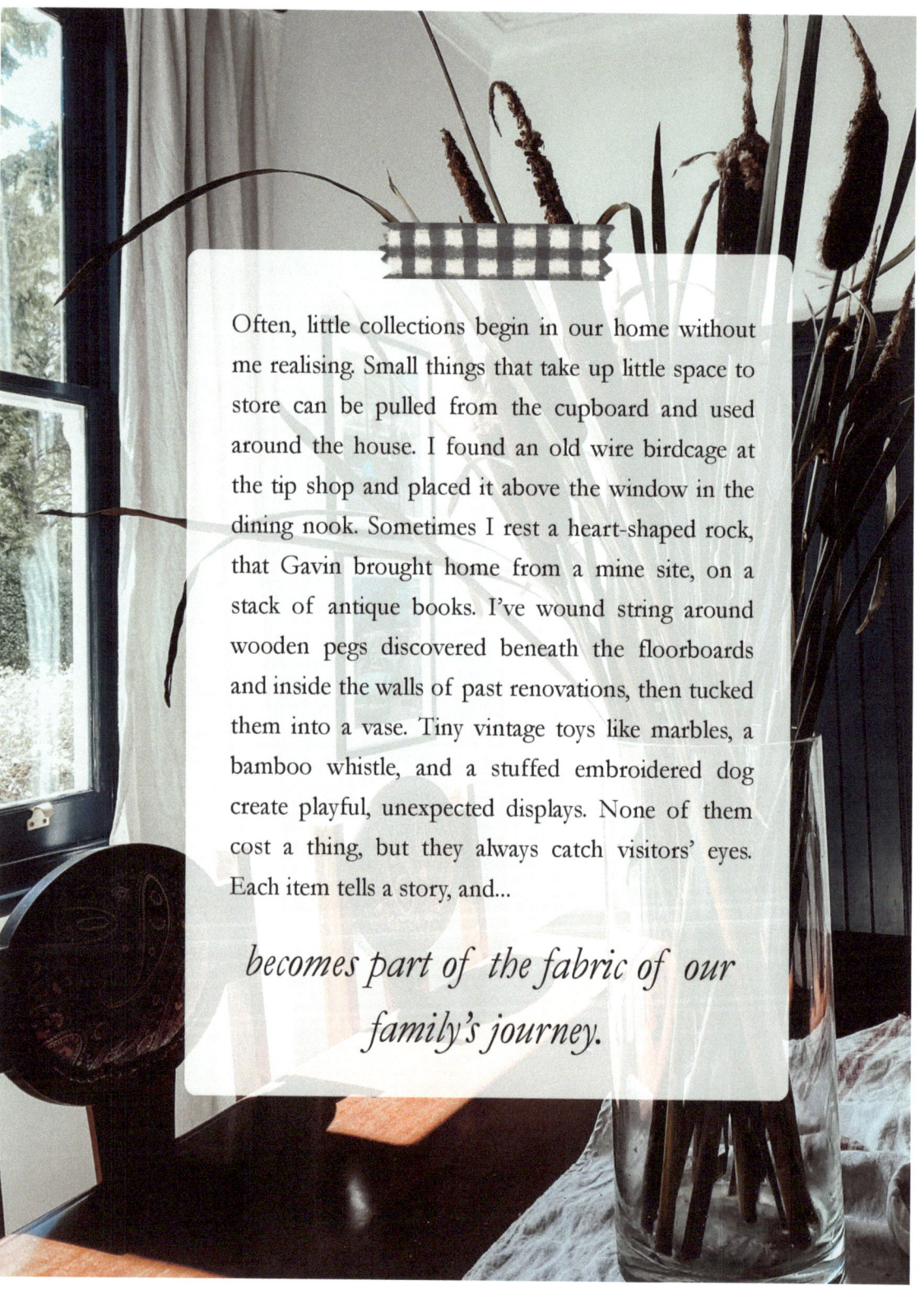

Often, little collections begin in our home without me realising. Small things that take up little space to store can be pulled from the cupboard and used around the house. I found an old wire birdcage at the tip shop and placed it above the window in the dining nook. Sometimes I rest a heart-shaped rock, that Gavin brought home from a mine site, on a stack of antique books. I've wound string around wooden pegs discovered beneath the floorboards and inside the walls of past renovations, then tucked them into a vase. Tiny vintage toys like marbles, a bamboo whistle, and a stuffed embroidered dog create playful, unexpected displays. None of them cost a thing, but they always catch visitors' eyes. Each item tells a story, and...

becomes part of the fabric of our family's journey.

QUICK TIP
TO STYLE VINTAGE FINDS

Choose pieces with a story, a patina, or a quirk. Mix them with your everyday essentials so they feel part of the home, not just on display.

VINTAGE FINDS FOR THE HOME

A THRIFTED PICNIC BASKET SITS ON TOP OF THE ARMOIRE | PERFECT FOR HIDING BULKY DOCUMENTS

My interior style is never complete without vintage and antique pieces. In days gone by, I chose them because they were affordable. At the time, antiques weren't fashionable and could be purchased for almost nothing, which was fortunate, because we had nothing. During the cottage renovation, I was lucky to have a budget that allowed for the purchase of French and English pieces to add to our auction finds.

However they've been acquired, old pieces always feature in our home. The uniqueness and charm they bring to a room is what makes our home feel individual. I usually purchase pieces for particular spaces but am drawn to anything versatile that can be used in different ways. Chests of drawers are a perfect example. I've used them as a TV stand, a hall table, a console and a vanity, not to mention their intended purpose of clothes storage. A bookcase can become kitchen storage, or a display spot in the living room. Old wardrobes make perfect linen storage when internal shelves are added. They're also a unique way to store brooms, the vacuum cleaner, and other household cleaning items. A tea trolley can double as a side table and a trunk used as an ottoman or coffee table.

LITTLE KEEPSAKE No 6
A tiny glass bottle, dug up from the garden bed behind the cottage. Empty now, but once it held something precious—just like the house that keeps it now.

When hunting for furniture to layer in, I gravitate towards pieces with sweet details and legs, especially turned legs or feet. Being able to see under a piece makes it feel less bulky in a room. I'm not afraid of an ugly finish either. Knobs can be changed, and paint can be updated or stripped. In fact, you can make a simple cabinet suit almost any aesthetic and find a place for it in any room.

Stools are another collectible I use around the cottage. When not pulled up as a side table in the lounge or functioning as a bedside, they become additional seating at the dining table or a tiny coffee table on the porch. Among other favourites I keep in my stash, and look out for when shopping, are antique bottles, especially amber or tiny decorative ones. These look wonderful en masse, as a vase for a single bloom or as candle holders on the dining table.

Likewise, a collection of vintage plates never goes astray in our house. A bundle of square plates purchased for five dollars lines the top of the opening between the kitchen and living room. My plate rack rotates constantly: seasonal plates mixed with old favourites to change up the look: blue transferware for summer, Milton autumn plates that belonged to my grandmother, green cabbage knock-offs and bunnies for spring, and my collection of red vintage and Christmas plates for the holiday season. If we're entertaining and I want to create a certain vibe on the table, I simply take them down and use them.

Plates: the new bunting, bringing seasonal joy without the dust

A pair of wooden ducks to remind me of our farm life

FAVOURITE VINTAGE TREASURES

These pieces are displayed sparingly throughout our home and rotated in and out of use with other items I store until needed. I stack everything in a single two-shelf cupboard, where it's easy to access. I don't need a mountain of décor to create a look. Mixing my limited options with modern lamps, art, decorative bowls, trays, and vases keeps me creative all year round. My goal is to create a curated, lived-in look, not to turn our house into a museum.

Items I Love to Collect

- sets of floral teacups and plates
- antique jugs and pitchers
- wooden shoe lasts
- ceramic vessels
- glass vases
- linen table napkins and cloths
- vintage canisters and cake tins
- authentic tin signs
- any art with a gilt frame
- black and white family photos
- treasures from my family, such as watercolours, embroidery and books
- old books
- vintage birdcages
- trunks
- little stools
- gilt mirrors

Gold ornate frames are a must

vintage toys make perfect shelf moments

Quick Tip
For Mixing Metals

Pick one dominant metal finish, then layer in one or two complementary tones in smaller accents. This keeps the look intentional while adding depth and interest.

A CASE FOR MIXING HARDWARE

GILT AND BRASS AT THE
FARMHOUSE | LIFE'S TOO SHORT FOR
MATCHY-MATCHY

One of my favourite design choices is mixing metals in taps and hardware. While some people swear by a cohesive, streamlined look, where every fixture is matte black or aged brass, I find charm in a more layered, collected aesthetic. After all, most old homes weren't built with matchy-matchy design in mind. Budgets dictated choices, and fixtures were often chosen for their practicality.

It was clear that the original owners of the cottage had the luxury of an 'indoor kitchen', but it wasn't a showpiece with plumbing. It was a room with a fireplace and kitchen furniture, a hardworking space. The ornate touches in our home were reserved for the more public "show-off" rooms, think intricate mantel details and decorative door hardware. Even those were chosen with budget and availability in mind, so they don't all match. The doors still had their heavy cast iron rim locks, paired with a mix of porcelain and metal knobs, but the builder had installed some locks upside down, most likely because the right type wasn't available in the early settlement. A few doors had porcelain handles, while others featured metal, choices that were clearly made for convenience and cost, not design.

LITTLE KEEPSAKE No 7
A silver teaspoon from a vintage set gifted to us on our wedding day, but never too precious to use.

Our farmhouse leaned toward cohesion with an occasional surprise, but at the cottage, I've embraced this eclectic approach to hardware and fittings, balancing copper, antique brass, and a touch of black throughout. The new handles vary in the same way as the old. Some feature porcelain knobs, others are crafted from wood or metal, yet the overall look feels cohesive and authentic in its collected charm. This mix-and-match style enhances the cottage's original quirks, giving the impression of a home pieced together over time.

> *"Mixing metals is a little like setting a table for new friends. You want everyone to get along, even if their views might differ."*

My failsafe approach is to choose two or three finishes I love and let them appear more than once, so the eye recognises them as part of the story. Warm brass might sit alongside cool nickel, with copper making a cameo appearance in the background. One finish takes the lead, the others simply add depth, like supporting characters in a well-told tale, or accessories on an outfit.

Metal accessories play a part too: a brass based lamp, the hinges on a door or a cast iron doorstop all add a tiny cohesive details to a room.

When repeated with care, the variety feels collected and natural. It's the hallmark of a well thought-out interior.

Copper, antique brass and matt black in the laundry area

FINDING THE HEART OF A HOME

The inspiration and ideas that bring
rooms to life

FIELD NOTES *No 3*

Photographed 9 June 2024

AN INVITATION TO STEP INSIDE |
ORIGINAL PORCELAIN DOORKNOB

A porcelain knob, smoothed by hands over many years, reminds me that finding the heart of a home begins with a door left ajar, and the courage to walk through it.

FINDING THE HEART OF A HOME

The inspiration and ideas that bring rooms to life

Inspiration can be a tricky thing, even for a serial decorator like me who spends a good deal of time immersed in decorating. Sometimes, despite the countless ideas swirling in my mind, I find myself unsure where to start or which choice to make. The inspiration simply isn't there. While I often remind myself, "It's only paint," the fear of making the wrong choice can feel paralysing. I'll look at samples for hours, make a decision, then start second-guessing it. Some days, the amount of choice feels more like a curse than a blessing, especially when fabric swatches are covering every surface. (Yes, it did take me a year to choose a slipcover for the sofa, but don't judge.) The volume of thoughts can be overwhelming to my organisation-loving brain.

But, as I've learned from writing novels, the best thing to do when inspiration won't come is step away, take a breather, and let creativity find me. Ideas have a way of sneaking up in the oddest places, like the shower. (Some of my best plot twists have emerged while shampooing my hair.) Creativity builds on itself, too. Once I begin, new ideas start to flow. One small decision, leads to another. I might start with a single sample and, before long, I'm envisioning an entire room around it. The act of doing unlocks more than inspiration; it creates momentum.

In the next section, you'll discover a few of my favourite sources of inspiration, my methods for putting a room together over time, and a few little tricks. These aren't groundbreaking or new, but they're tried and tested and, I turn to them often.

QUICK TIP
FOR EMBRACING ERA

Georgian homes favour balance and symmetry. Echo this indoors with paired furniture and classic panelling. A few well-placed antiques will feel right at home.

THE CONVICT HOUSE
circa 1847

THE ERA OF A HOME

PROVAND'S LORDSHIP | 1471 | VISITED BY MARY QUEEN OF SCOTS

Every house has a story to tell and, if you listen closely, it will guide you. I know that may sound odd, but I believe a house reveals itself when you take the time to look. The design and architectural details (or the lack of them) can serve as a starting point. These elements shape my choices in colour, decor, and design—especially since I aim to honour the home's heritage. The aim isn't restoring every detail so we're living in a museum, but rather, to let the original features guide my choices. A home with sash windows and deep skirting boards suits a more traditional or heritage-inspired feel, even when styled in a modern way. Working with what's there nearly always results in a cohesive space. In Australia, it's common to find mid-century modern homes with clean lines, large windows, and open-plan layouts. These lend themselves to a more minimalist or Scandinavian-inspired aesthetic, where light wood tones, tapered furniture legs, and pared-back styling shine. Meanwhile, the California bungalows of the 1930's call for something warmer and more layered. Their wide porches, timber fretwork, and low-pitched roofs are enhanced with vintage lighting and textured fabrics. The more you work with a home's style, the more cohesive it will feel.

LITTLE KEEPSAKE No 8
A key without a door, but a thousand stories to tell.
After finding it in the laundry door, I wondered at the
hands who'd twisted the key over the past century.

At Blackbird Cottage, those clues weren't always obvious. The house had been altered over time, and some of its original Georgian features had vanished or been compromised. But the ones that remained like the small-paned windows, timber floors, and deep skirting boards gave me enough to work with. I let those architectural cues guide my choices in trim, colour palette, and layout. Even details like adding corner rosettes felt like a way to reintroduce what the cottage may once have had.

The layers of wallpaper in the house influenced my decisions, too. While many Australian cottages favour a white and timber aesthetic, our cottage seemed to call for something richer, a nod to Victorian styles. The cottage cried out for us to bring colour and pattern back, blending heritage with a modern touch. What we removed needed to be replaced.

It seems strange to me to strip a home of its character under the banner of modernisation or to change its inherent personality. The quirks, the materials, even the so-called shortcomings speak to the time in which a house was built. They're often exactly why you fall for a home in the first place. Styles change, materials change, but those features, whether ornate or modest, deserve to be celebrated, not concealed. Yes, modernise and renovate for thermal efficiency and cost saving, but keep the spirit of the home and layer it into your aesthetic. That's the key to good design.

The Convict House we lived in for a time offers a perfect example. Its decor leaned classic, but it felt a little uninspired. The off white mixed with brown and 80's slate tiles flattened the rooms and didn't show off their beauty. The decor made the house feel cold.

I pored over historical palettes and chose a blue for downstairs rooms, a colour rooted in the period. This blue deepened to periwinkle in the kitchen and sunroom. I removed the dated Austrian blinds, replacing the front blinds with custom Roman shades in a heritage print. The look was updated but a blend of old and new. Had we removed the turned staircase or concealed the original timber ceilings, the soul of the house would have disappeared. The joy of living in an old home lies in leaning into its era, not erasing it.

How Blackbird Cottage looked in the 1920s

OTHER PEOPLE'S HOMES

PLOTTING IDEAS FOR WINDOW BOXES |
DEAN VILLAGE, EDINBURGH

Over the years, I've found inspiration in the homes of friends and loved ones. I remember, back in the 1990s, one of my friends papered her hall in a gorgeous Sanderson floral wallpaper overflowing with burgundy blooms. At the time, we weren't financially able to embrace such a bold choice, and I would never copy a friend, no matter how flattering that might be. But I admired her choice and it planted a seed. Decades later, when I was selecting wallpaper, I thought back to her hallway and how she'd carried those colours throughout her home, in paint choices and accessories. It was a lesson in cohesion and flow.

I'm endlessly inspired by visiting heritage homes, too. On a trip to the UK, we stopped at a tea room in York with such beautiful wall treatments that I considered changing the colour palette of the cottage to a shade of plaster pink. Then I fell for a deep green-black shade called Obsidian, when we visited a tiny antique shop in Kingsbridge.

My point is, every place offered something, from cosy nooks in tiny cottages to grand rooms with soaring ceilings and intricate details. One cottage had such low ceilings, complete with 14th-century oak beams, that ducking downstairs became a full-body sport. I came back full of ideas for layering furniture to make the most of our spaces. I wanted to celebrate the darker, snug corners. That trip helped me see our cottage with new eyes.

On a wet afternoon at Thurnham Hall in Lancaster, I found myself studying the interplay of pattern and colour in the main hall. The warm timber, textiles, and graceful proportions reminded me how much I draw inspiration from the way others live in their homes. Every trip away from the cottage leaves me with more than just photographs. It gives me ideas. These are the details that weave their way into Blackbird Cottage.

NATURE AS INSPIRATION

THIS VIEW CHOSE THE PALETTE | I SIMPLY OBEYED

A cottage garden with its vibrant colours, the texture of old gnarled wood, or a patterned linen cushion—all have influenced my style over the years. I'm drawn to the way nature combines colours and textures effortlessly, even when the choice is subconscious. If it looks good in nature, it will look good in my home. So, I suppose it was not by chance that the greens and yellows of my local environment have played such an important role in the interior of the cottage.

Back in the early '90s, we moved to the house we'll call The Bush House. We were were desperate for an extra bedroom and land (as was often the case for us), so a house in the bush seemed like a good idea. It wasn't us, though. We stayed only a couple of years. That was the season when botanical prints crept indoors, arriving as wallpaper borders in gentle blues and greens. They were pretty, and they nodded to the nature beyond the windows, though in truth they didn't quite belong to the style of house we were living in.

It was at The Bush House I began to notice what lay beyond the glass. A colour palette of dark eucalyptus green, soft tan from the rock wall in the backyard, and the clear blue of agapanthus soon followed. Even the vertical blinds I didn't like surrendered to the outside world when thrown open wide, allowing the tree canopy to take centre stage.

At Green Gate Farm we found that moving the kitchen from the side of the house to the back, revealed a breathtaking view of the hills beyond. This view inspired the deep charcoal paint that acted as a 'frame' around the windows. The view was the driver for our design decision to put the kitchen sink in front of the window. Nature has a way of guiding me, and I happily follow.

SIMPLE SECRETS FOR A HOME THAT FLOWS

OUR DOLLHOUSE | ARCHITECT DESIGNED | 1940'S BRICK

Our third home, the one I affectionately call The Dollhouse, was a dreamy 1940s two-storey brick, complete with a central staircase, symmetrical windows and a chimney that reached for the sky. It had a terrazzo floor in the bathroom and a small hidden room off the bedroom that became our son's. The house was architect-designed and similar in style to Cape Cod homes. It had a wonderful feel and buckets of potential.

As a child, I told my mother I'd buy that house one day. (I don't recall saying that, but Mum reminded me after we purchased.) The Dollhouse remains the only house I've ever regretted selling. Maybe it was because the house felt so grand, being the antithesis of the bungalow my family lived in, or perhaps because it spoke to my old-soul heart. I was school friends with a girl who lived there and remember a sleepover where we performed a play, using the large built-in wardrobe as the stage. That room would one day become our bedroom. Over the course of our friendship, there were dinners in the dining room and breakfasts at the banquet in the kitchen. It was a perfect family home. By the time we bought the house, I'd already weathered a few decorating disasters, but with each house, I learned more. The Dollhouse marked a turning point. I began to realise that creating a cohesive home wasn't about copying a magazine spread, it was about weaving together pieces that felt like us.

Over many lazy Sunday mornings in bed, poring over magazines while the children snuggled up beside me watching cartoons, I pieced together the tips and ideas that would eventually evolve into my style, the one you see at Blackbird Cottage today.

Back then, I leaned into a familiar muse—Laura Ashley. Her palettes and patterns made sense to me. I'd already worn her dresses, so why not let her influence my interiors? Not literally, of course. Having Laura Ashley do a design consult at my home, while a dream come true, was never going to happen. Firstly, it would never have been in our budget, and secondly, the great lady had passed on around ten years before we owned The Dollhouse.

I couldn't afford authentic Laura Ashley fabrics or custom furnishings, but I could certainly emulate the feel. I chose buttery yellows and soft blues, painting the kitchen walls a Wedgwood blue and crafting Roman blinds in a similar floral print. When Spode-style tiles were out of reach, I hand-painted my own using porcelain paint and a steady hand. I saved for a month to buy Designers Guild and Laura Ashley wallpaper friezes for the bedrooms.

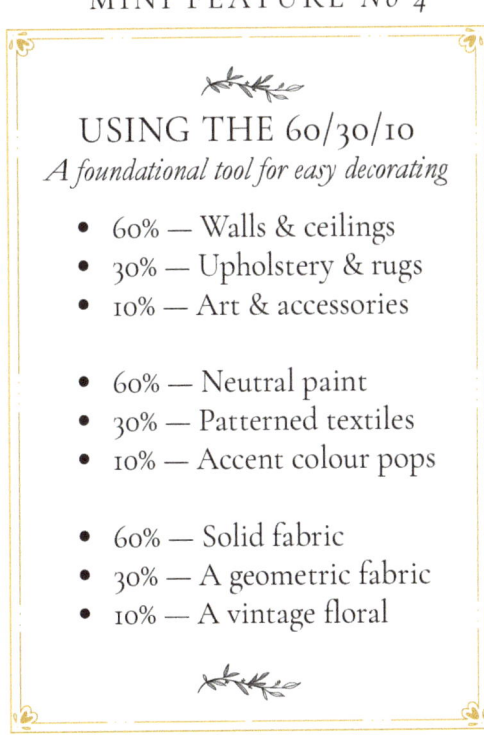

MINI FEATURE No 4

USING THE 60/30/10
A foundational tool for easy decorating

- 60% — Walls & ceilings
- 30% — Upholstery & rugs
- 10% — Art & accessories

- 60% — Neutral paint
- 30% — Patterned textiles
- 10% — Accent colour pops

- 60% — Solid fabric
- 30% — A geometric fabric
- 10% — A vintage floral

What I didn't realise at the time was that I was following a design principle that would later become a cornerstone of how I create rooms: balance, repetition and restraint. I was using a basic cohesive colour scheme and applying it throughout our home.

My process was simple, and if I'd known what I do now, I would have added variations in tone, shade and texture—but even then, I was on the right track. The scheme made our home feel more 'put together' than either of the other homes we'd so far owned. That idea was called the 60/30/10 Rule

the 60/30/10 rule

is simple, flexible and effective, which is perfect for someone who wants cohesion in their interiors without overthinking every detail.

I use this strategy in every room of Blackbird Cottage. My 60% is cream on the ceilings, trim and the walls of the kitchen and bathroom. The 30% is grounded in an earthy green, used on walls below the dado and reflected again in wallpapers, china and subtle tones of art. The final 10% brings joy: mustard, blue and a hint of pink. Because the colours repeat throughout, I can move pieces between rooms without worrying if they'll 'go.' That, to me, is the essence of effortless style.

ADAPTING LAURA ASHLEY'S PALETTE

the red thread

As my confidence grew, I began paying closer attention to how our rooms relate—not just within their four walls, but in how they flow from one to the next. Two ideas that help guide me now are sightlines and the Red Thread. Sightlines are what you see when you look from one room into the next. If the tones, textures or shapes clash, even subtly, it can feel unsettling without you quite knowing why. That's where the Red Thread theory comes in. The Red Thread is a repeated visual element that connects your spaces. Think of it as a string weaving from room to room, visually linking elements to help your mind make sense of the space. Items don't need to match, and the same element doesn't need to appear in every room (lest things start to feel contrived) but elements should echo throughout.

These are the details that make a house feel intentional, even when a budget or your season of life, demands you work with what you already have. It's not about perfection; it's about familiarity, consistency, and layering meaning through repetition.

Without planning it, this table setting followed the 60/30/10 rule: soft blue dominates, green balances, and a hint of pink lifts it just enough to catch the eye. A mix of vintage and new with second hand plates, modern cutlery, and a cloth I stitched in under an hour, coming together without ceremony.

LESSONS LEARNED IN CREATING A HOME

A WORK IN PROGRESS | THE NEW LIVING ROOM | DEC 2023

One of the most freeing lessons I've learned over decades of home renovating, is that a home doesn't need a designer label to feel elevated and beautiful. Some of my favourite corners are a blend of secondhand finds, hand-me-downs, and the occasional splurge. Being able to source a similar cushion or fabric for half the cost can be a lot of fun. It's the balance that gives a room its charm: the rough beside the refined, the practical alongside the precious. It's not how much you paid for a sofa or lamp. The expensive things are nice, but they're not always necessary.

Another lesson I've learned, time and time again, is that creating a home takes patience. I used to believe I could transform a space overnight with a new colour on the walls or adding extra cushions to the sofa. Sometimes that works, but more often, it doesn't hit the mark. The best rooms evolve slowly. They need time for gathering the right pieces, like the painting that finds you at a market or the antique that fits a spot perfectly. I've learned to wait for the right piece instead of settling for "good enough." In the early days, I'd buy things to fill a gap, only to regret it later. Now I know that leaving a corner empty for a while often leads to something better, a find that feels like it's meant to be, one that makes the room feel whole without forcing it.

Another lesson I've learned is not to fear change once a room is "done." Even my favourite spaces need a refresh now and then. A new throw on the bed, a painting swapped to a different wall, or furniture shuffled to suit how we live are all acceptable. Small changes breathe fresh life into a home. Rooms should grow with us, not stay frozen in time.

So, I began to use these lessons and embrace a sequence and, once I did, the interiors of our future homes and flip houses felt cohesive, practical, and timeless. By implementing this system, my creativity blossomed. I began to see homes fully completed in my mind and it became easier for me to picture items that would suit a room and live effortlessly together. It's my approach to decorating, and one that could work for you, too.

a word on mood boards

For some, a mood board is an abstract concept, an evocation of feeling or atmosphere. For others, it's a curated gallery of inspiration images. For me, the mood board is far more practical: it is a testing ground. It helps me see how the shapes, colours and textures will speak to each other once they're in the room. Will the brass light fitting complement the curtain rod? Does this rug hold its own beside the lamp I love?

Sometimes my board is **digital**, built from online finds. Other times, it's a **tactile** mess of fabric swatches, timber samples and paint chips spread out across the floor. It's rarely final, but it's always helpful. It keeps me grounded when I'm tempted to follow a passing trend or add one more "maybe" to the cart.

It's worth noting that while the mood board helps create my plan, that plan isn't set in stone. My designs evolve because of budget, availability or simply because I fall in love with something unexpected. But that's where the magic lives. The mood board is my start line, not my destination. The mood board keeps me in check. It's like a stylish best friend who doesn't let me buy the wrong rug.

MY LAYERED APPROACH TO DECORATING

Before we begin, I need to clarify that the next steps are the general order I follow when selecting materials and finishes to build a scheme. When it comes to the hands-on part of decorating, I work from the top of the room down—starting with ceilings and walls, finishing with the floors, then adding the previously chosen furniture, soft furnishings and hardware. This approach means finished floors don't end up splattered with paint or wallpaper glue.

STEP ONE - *floors*

Whether it's rugs, tiles, carpet or timber, the floor sets the tone of the room. It's a prominent structural feature that can make or break the interior. Choosing a floor finish is a major decision. It's expensive, and can be inconvenient to replace, so making the right choice for our home and interior always mattered.

Tackling the major renovation of the cottage meant setting aside a budget for the floor, but this hasn't been the case in other homes we've owned. We've also rarely had the luxury of an empty house to work with.

At The Colourful House, we moved our furniture into the alfresco and stayed in a caravan for a week. At the Terrace Cottage, we tiptoed over floor joists and juggled unpacked boxes so the carpenter could replace a rotten floor.

Liming white on the cottage floors

Painted floors at Green Gate Farm

At Green Gate Farm, I wanted the renovated dairy's floor to be as much a feature as the view beyond the windows. I painted a simple chequerboard pattern directly onto the concrete, using the same soft beige as the walls for the 'tiles' and crisp green in between. The effect was instantly fresh and cheerful, which tied the space together while adding a subtle nod to traditional country kitchens.

Green Gate Farm was trickier. The floor was a mismatch of patched and original boards, different in width and tone. In an ideal world, we would have put in a new floor, but there was no budget for that, so I had to find creative ways to make the existing boards work with the look I wanted.

Initially, I stained the floor with Black Japan, the traditional Victorian stain used in the halls and bedroom. It seemed like a good idea at the time, but in reality, the dark finish constantly looked dusty and dirty. It drove me nuts. Determined to find a better solution, I started researching the possibility of painting the floor instead. To unify the space with the rest of our home (because I'd already decorated and doing it again wasn't on my agenda), I chose a custom paving paint tinted in a pale beige-white—one I matched to the trim colour from our paint cards. The transformation was remarkable. The result was bright, fresh and cohesive, turning what had been an eyesore into a standout feature of the house. This project taught me that even when the floor isn't the first thing you tackle, it can still become an integral part of the overall scheme. Sometimes, thinking outside the box with flooring leads to unexpected and delightful results.

As a complete aside, if I was ever to paint a floor again, and I would, a light colour is the way to go. It won't show dust, is no dirtier than a dark floor and looks wonderful with many decorating styles.

MINI FEATURE No 5

FLOORING FOR A COTTAGE FEEL
The base layer for cottage charm

- Timber planks: the wider the better
- Room sized rug: Jute or a Persian style pattern
- Engineered timber
- Painted floorboards
- Checkerboard tile
- Painted checkerboard
- Mosaic or penny round tile
- Terracotta, matt travertine or flagstone look tile
- French lay tile

STEP TWO - *fabric, pattern & textiles*

Before I even contemplated wall colours for the cottage, I was knee-deep in collecting samples. I had a vague idea that green would play a starring role, but the exact shade didn't reveal itself until the wallpaper samples arrived. I lived with those samples taped to the walls for weeks while I primed and caulked gaps, walking by them dozens of times a day. Eventually, the perfect patterns spoke to me, and once I'd chosen the wallpapers for each bedroom, the paint colours for the hall and living room naturally followed, tying everything together like a well-orchestrated symphony.

Over the course of the renovation, I amassed an impressive collection of fabric swatches for sofa slipcovers, blinds, curtains and cushions. I ordered a few at a time in colours I thought would complement the wallpapers. Unsurprisingly, many looked nothing like they had on my laptop screen and were promptly discarded. Others simply didn't work in the room's lighting. But after narrowing down my choices, I began layering textures of wicker, rattan and linen accessories, while considering the existing furniture and ensuring everything played nicely together.

Yes, most companies charge for samples (or at least the postage), but trust me, it's worth every penny. The alternative? Spending a fortune to return ill-fitting fixtures or ending up stuck with curtains in a shade you'll forever resent. And no one wants that. This is why choosing some fabrics or wallpapers before you set foot in the paint store is essential. You can take those swatches and have them colour-matched to paint at a later date but, as I learned the hard way, it's tricky to match a fabric to a paint once it's on the walls.

STEP THREE-*paint*

Once my fabrics, wallpapers and textures are locked in, I turn my attention to paint. For over a decade now, my go-to wall colour has been a warm neutral paired with a richer trim. I usually default to Dulux Natural White, but for the cottage, the colour felt too stark—a bit too "white." So, I did some digging and found an Australian paint company with an intriguing online range. Their customer service rep convinced me to try a shade called C.R.E.A.M. Yes, it's as simple as it sounds: a creamy, rich tone with softness and depth. It wasn't yellow like most creamy whites, which was a relief, but stepping out of my comfort zone still made me nervous. Was I about to drown my cottage in a colour that screamed 1970s grandma's bungalow? Thankfully, no. The shade is perfection: warm and inviting in the living room, bright in the kitchen and even clean and crisp as trim. Though that first roller stroke on the wall made my heart pound. And I'm not usually one to panic over paint.

For contrast, I chose an earthy green for below the dado rail, as well as the skirting boards and architraves. The same shade appears in the guest room as a deep green wallpaper, tying the spaces together seamlessly.

With the main colours in place, I add accent tones to bring dimension and depth. As mentioned, I swear by the 60/30/10 rule. It's the secret to interiors that feel both cohesive and interesting—balanced, but never boring. The little pops around our home are the things I switch when I need a refresh. A mustard throw might be swapped for a pale blue one in summer. A dark velvet cushion becomes a sunny yellow or light linen. The accents are interchangeable, but the base remains the same.

LITTLE KEEPSAKE *No 9*
A paint brush, coated from many applications of my favourite creamy white. The fresh start we've brushed onto the cottage walls wasn't only for the house.

STEP FOUR - *furniture*

The next step after choosing colours is furniture. Sometimes I work with what I have; other times, I purchase new, or new-to-us. We brought a handful of pieces from Green Gate Farm, some for their sentimental value, others because I knew they'd suit the cottage. But, as with any move, there was culling. Several pieces simply didn't make the final edit. I have no qualms about letting pieces go. It's only furniture. Selling frees up cash to buy items that suit a new home.

Before bringing any piece into a room, I assess the space, not just physically, but by asking what the room needs to do, and whether what I own can meet that need. I mentally map out where each piece belongs, guided by function first.

There were a couple of painful decisions with pieces I loved but couldn't make work. Our dining table was too long, and the leather lounge suite? We knew it wouldn't fit through the door. I put them into storage until the time came to decide. In the end, I sold them without guilt. I was happy to see them find new homes.

Perfectly suited for the cottage, the red cabinet was a 'yes'

An antique sofa that didn't survive the cull

Only a few old pieces made it into each room. I stopped trying to recreate past layouts and started listening to what the space needed. The house became lighter, and less about holding onto the past.

But it's not all about old. At Blackbird Cottage, I use modern pieces to temper the abundance of antiques. I look for ways to maximise storage without sacrificing style and, by the time moving day arrives, I know where each item will go, saving everyone's backs in the process.

Too bulky for the living room, but perfect for the kitchen

Of course, not everything works straight away. Sometimes, despite the planning, a piece just doesn't look right in its chosen spot and needs to either move or be gone from the house. I've learned to live with said piece for a while, mull it over, and then make a change. This approach has saved me heartache over the loss of a piece I loved.

Our colonial cedar cabinet was one such headache. We'd bought it for the space beside the living room chimney, but its size and colour dominated the room, no matter how I styled it. For nearly a year, I debated painting it, and even selling it. Eventually, the solution became clear: it wasn't the cabinet that was the problem, but its location. We moved it to the dining area, where it has space to breathe. It's role as a home for glassware, extra china and wine storage feels more in keeping in the nook and the cabinet finally feels at home. Perfection doesn't happen in a day, which is why I hold off on adding smaller pieces until a room feels almost complete. This approach prevents unnecessary clutter and gives me time to find the right piece, whether it's new or secondhand. It's slower, but it's a process I love. After all, a room should evolve naturally, not feel like it's been filled in a single shopping spree.

STEP FIVE-*lighting*

There's a design "rule" that every room needs at least three sources of light: overhead, ambient or task lighting, and accent lights. With my overall scheme taking shape, lighting becomes the icing on my design cake, a final flourish that ties everything together. For me, lights are like the hats of an outfit: an opportunity to express individuality, embrace functionality and add beauty. They're also delightfully changeable, making it easy to switch things up as often as my budget allows or my mood demands.

Quality lights don't have to cost the earth. They can be sourced online for far less than buying from physical shops. The only caveat is that many lights come from overseas, so it's important to check the sockets and wiring meet the standards of your country.

At the cottage, my goal was cohesive lighting with a traditional feel, achieved through thoughtful repetition of elements. With space at a premium, I wanted everything to flow, so I chose a mix of overhead pendants and wall sconces, accented with shades in linen, milk glass and rattan, all featuring playful scalloped or pleated details. These touches lend character while maintaining harmony across the rooms. To add a little sparkle, the hardware is finished in brass-look metal or burnished gold. It's just the right amount of bling. Admittedly, the overhead lights see little use. While functional, they serve more of an aesthetic purpose.

In the bedrooms, delicate scalloped rattan pendants hang on brass chains above the beds, a nod to traditional pendant placement. Wall sconces and table lamps provide soft night lighting and reading light.

LITTLE KEEPSAKE No 10
This light isn't original, but it's similar to the one that hung here long ago. Some details are worth replicating, even if they need to be reimagined in a modern way.

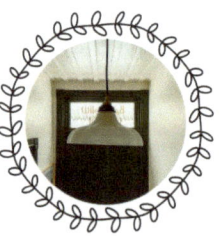

In the bathrooms, petite milk glass pendants illuminate the vanity and sink areas, while downlights are useful when doing laundry or putting on makeup. Brass wall sconces flank each side of the rangehood in the kitchen, and a large custom pendant creates drama in our dining nook.

At the cottage, it's the wall sconces and table lamps that do the heavy lifting. Sconces provide reading light in the bedrooms, while lamps scattered through the kitchen, office and living spaces offer ambient and task lighting. I have an enduring soft spot for lamps because they're versatile, timeless and adaptable to any style. Pleated and rattan shades add a cosy, layered warmth that makes each space feel inviting.

Lighting is one of the most transformative layers in design. It's the moment where function and flair collide. In the cottage, it's not just about illuminating the room. It's about creating atmosphere, telling a story, and adding the perfect finishing touch to the scheme. Below, you'll see examples of the lighting types I use in every scheme. Layering different light sources also lets me shift the atmosphere throughout the day—bright and energising in the morning, soft and golden by evening.

Lighting Types

Overhead
The hero of the room: practical, but never dull. Think chandeliers with charm or pendants that draw the eye upward and set the tone.

Ambient
These lights, like a scalloped sconce or one tucked into a shelf, add personality and charm without shouting.

Accent
Think table lamps on a sideboard or a lamp next to a favourite chair. These are perfect for cosy evenings.

Task
From a lamp by the laundry sink to a focused pendant over the bench, task lighting brings clarity to daily moments.

It's the little lights scattered throughout the cottage that make it feel like home—soft, warm, and working their magic without fuss.

STEP SIX - *accessories*

Accessories are the final layer, the red thread that pulls a room together and, finding the balance between styled and cluttered can be a delicate art, especially when you're not a stylist or designer, just someone decorating your home to suit your own taste. Some pieces work in a space, while others, no matter how beautiful, don't quite fit.

Personal taste plays a big role in the accessories and accents I use in the cottage. What looks stunning in my home might not translate elsewhere, and something that feels perfect on the shop floor can fall flat once it's unpacked and sitting in my lounge room. Finding the right accessories and creating layers is one of the true joys of decorating. It gives me the chance to tweak, rearrange and experiment until the room feels just right, like a place I genuinely want to spend time in. It's what gives our cottage that homely feel, the illusion that we've lived here for years, when that's not the reality. Choosing and styling an item might not be immediately noticed by guests, but it adds to the feeling I want to create, the story I'm trying to tell.

I keep my seasonal décor minimal but meaningful. In autumn, dried twigs in vintage bottles take centre stage, while in spring, delicate floral dishes make their annual debut. Space is limited, so everything I choose must earn its place by being beautiful, functional—or ideally, both. When it comes to styling, simplicity is key for me. A single oversized piece can make a striking statement, while too many small items risk creating visual chaos. I like to group accessories in odd numbers, varying heights and textures to create interest. Books and trays are my secret weapons, adding depth and cohesion.

LITTLE KEEPSAKE *No 11*
Once the keeper on the bedroom door, now a paperweight in my office. Decorative pieces don't have to be new, or cost the earth to be beautiful

Seasonal decor is like playing dress-ups in your house. It's fun to mark the passing months with small, joyful changes that make everyday corners feel fresh. Especially when you achieve the vibe without descending into kitsch or tacky.

Colour palette is my starting point for new finds. In our home, timber and marble feel natural, and the cottage's charm lends itself to big, bendy branches and organic shapes. Of course, trial and error is part of the process. When we first moved in, I recreated our beloved gallery wall of family photos—a feature that's followed us from house to house. But after a few months, I realised it wasn't working. The frames felt too heavy, the arrangement too busy. Eventually, I took it down, sold the frames, and tucked the photos into albums. Now, one black-and-white family portrait hangs beside a window, and two small miniatures of our parents are displayed as visitors walk down the hall—a cleaner, calmer look that still honours our memories. In the kitchen, I've displayed a single photo of my grandmothers, who would love being there, as they were both extraordinary cooks. And my one concession to clutter, a plate rack Gavin built, is stuffed to the brim with seasonal plates and dishes. Layering accessories is an ongoing process, not a race. The joy is in the journey: whether it's remembering where an item came from, marvelling at the way it completes a vignette, or deciding it's time to part ways, accessories should enhance your home, not become a source of stress. They're there to bring beauty and personality, not endless dusting or storage headaches.

This layering of colours, objects and textures is how our home takes shape over time, with thought and feeling. In the pages ahead, you'll see this approach in action as we move room by room, uncovering the choices that went into the creation of each space in the cottage.

MINI FEATURE No 6

STYLING ITEMS FROM MY STASH
little treasures to bring charm to any room

- Books (old or new)
- Candles and candlesticks
- Vessels filled with twigs, branches or seasonal blooms
- Vintage plates
- Seasonal mugs
- Flat bowls
- Trays
- Marble
- Timber risers
- Ceramic houses
- Plants (real or faux)
- Heirloom pieces: glass marbles, old pegs, shoe lasts, embroidery
- Cloches
- Clocks
- Unusual shaped vases

THE COTTAGE THAT WAITED

A little house, overlooked by the world, waiting
for someone to notice her charms

FIELD NOTES No 4

Discovered May 22 2023

WALL, MAIN BEDROOM | 19TH CENTURY
LADIES' FASHION ADVERT
PRINTED IN BLACK INK ON NEWSPAPER

This elegantly dressed lady emerged during clean out. Part catalogue of ladies' fashion, part moment in time, her buttoned bodice survived under decades of wallpaper.

THE COTTAGE THAT WAITED

A little house overlooked by the world, waiting for someone to notice her charm

Gavin and I have always followed our instincts when buying homes. For us, it's often a single, magical viewing that seals the deal. That might sound impulsive, but if I walk into a house and feel that spark, I know it's the right move. Gavin is the same way. We're energised by potential, the promise of creating a home that's uniquely ours. As I wander through the rooms, I imagine how each space might function, picturing the changes we'd make and the life we'd build within those walls.

The feeling of connection with a house isn't something everyone experiences the same way. For some, it's a sense of calm that makes a place feel like home. It might be the particular light in a room, or simply an instinct that says, "this is the place." I've never been able to fully articulate the feeling, and it's often not in a house I'd expect to like but, when the right house gives me all the feels, I start picturing it as ours: family dinners, festive gatherings, cosy nights.

The story was different with Blackbird Cottage. I didn't feel that familiar, all-consuming love at first sight. Maybe it was because we were about to leave our farmhouse—a place so dear to my heart, where I thought we'd stay until we were old—and that parting felt like mourning. Maybe it was the stress of finding a new home amid everything else happening in my life. My heart wasn't really in house hunting. I was just going through the motions. Walking into the cottage for the first time, I could see challenges on a level we'd never tackled, like freezing cold rooms and crumbling chimneys I had no idea how to conquer.

Frankly, I wasn't sure we could do it. Yet, we put in an offer that first day, and as we visited the house again, the possibilities began to reveal themselves. I slowly realised this little cottage was reaching out, asking for a new lease on life. I started to see the charm hidden beneath the neglect, and the more we worked and planned, the more connected I felt. Each small discovery breathed life back into the cottage, transforming it from a rundown structure into something endearing.

In the process, Blackbird Cottage became more than a house; it started to feel like a place that could be home. As we peeled back layers of wallpaper and ripped up dusty carpets, I began noticing details I hadn't seen before. There was a grace to the worn edges—a beauty in the imperfections that spoke of history, and I was eager to learn it all. Blackbird Cottage seemed to reveal herself slowly: the floorboards softened from decades of use, preserved under layers of newspaper; the myriad styles of convict nails holding the walls together; a name etched into a window pane; and even a penny from 1913 that fell from inside a door jamb. It felt as if the cottage was waiting for us to prove our commitment before showing her true character.

After settlement, Gavin and I fell into a rhythm. He tackled the outdoors, helping with the heavier tasks inside that I couldn't manage alone. Over morning coffees on the verandah, we talked through our plans, making lists on my notes app and sketching out ideas. Together, we sourced plants for the garden and stacked shingles removed from the roof. We carefully dismantled features we wanted to preserve and worked out ways to replicate those too far gone to save.

And this house had original features in abundance: doors, hardware, windows, floors, ceilings and chimneys—all needing more than a touch of TLC. It was in that work that my love for the cottage began to grow. Every nail hammered, every board sanded, felt like a small act of devotion. We were building something special, piece by piece.

the charm beneath years of neglect

My initial thought was that the cottage we'd purchased had low, stifling ceilings—and I wasn't overly happy about that. Having lived with twelve-foot ceilings for many years, the prospect of feeling 'boxed in' could easily have been a deal breaker. As it turned out, I was wrong.

Discoloured by decades of nicotine and stained a dull amber, the ceilings looked beyond saving. We knew they were painted solid timber beneath the grime, but no ordinary cleaner could cut through the buildup. One of my followers suggested a forensic-grade product and, to our amazement, it worked. We watched years of residue drip away, revealing ceilings far higher than expected. Crafted in the style of early colonial homes, they featured board and batten with hand-routed detailing, each line cut with care. The routed effect is mirrored on the exterior weatherboards of the cottage, making it one step above its twin next door. The process left me short of breath each day—not from the cleaning agent or lack of fitness, but from the stench of lingering tobacco fumes. Still, as the wood became cleaner, the character of the ceiling began to emerge. We'd transformed something that was once oppressive into what would become a beautiful feature, once I completed the cosmetic work.

Over several weeks I painstakingly filled the gaps along the length of each batten in every room. The gap filler was messy no matter what technique I tried, but once finished, it was easier to envision how the ceilings would look with a fresh coat of paint.

Gavin cut tiny individual timber strips to slot into the spaces between the battens. This created a finished look where the new plaster met the ceiling and, once painted, the strips became part of the ceiling profile.

Primed and finished in soft cream paint, the ceilings highlight the care and thought that went into this modest home. They have a cosy, yet custom feel that modern plasterboard simply can't replicate.

preserving heritage windows

One of the things I adore about the cottage is the original King Billy Pine windows. Each hand-blown glass pane, dotted with air bubbles, tells a story of its own. One pane contains etched names of past inhabitants, another was scarred by a tiny bullet hole. The windows were painted shut when we began work, and I understood why: painting windows shut kept out the draughts, and the house was incredibly cold. But they still needed restoring.

I began researching ways to repair them. Most of the quotes were eye-wateringly high, but the carpenter who'd worked on the farm renovation came to the rescue, showing me how to dismantle each window. This task was easier than expected as the cottage windows are simply two panels inserted into the frame and held in place with a timber bead. They have no cords to raise them, and so, can be popped in and out. This style of 'Poverty Window' predates the sash windows we're familiar with today. Therefore, keeping the integrity of the windows, and the way they operate, felt important.

Repairing windows was a task I never imagined myself doing, but I enjoyed it. There was much satisfaction in knowing I'd completed the job myself, giving what were once rotting windows a few more years of life. The repaired windows in the front rooms aren't thermally efficient, but the broken panes have been replaced and the rot removed. We can now open them to let the fresh air in, and with the addition of dainty sash lifts to hold them up, they're both functional and pretty. It was worth the effort to save them. They're a rare find, and the addition of decorative architraves around the frames has brought new charm to the original features.

By contrast, the windows in the living room and main bedroom were beyond repair. Despite my best efforts, we bit the bullet and commissioned new windows crafted to replicate the originals. Yes, I loved the old glass with its quirks and history, but the thicker laminated panes and sturdy construction of the replica windows eliminated drafts. The cottage is warmer and our electricity bills are loving it too.

a hand-sawn timber floor

The initial cleanup involved peeling back layers of crumbling linoleum, musty carpet and newspapers thinned by time. The old articles and sporting pages weren't merely an historical timestamp. We often stopped to laugh at the images of the time, a welcome distraction from crawling about in dust.

Newspapers from the 1920s lined the floor along the hall, trapping decades of filth. We shovelled it into wheelbarrows and dumped it in the garden. Every day, we left the house looking more like nineteenth-century chimney sweeps than renovators. But our labour was rewarded when we reached the bottom layer and discovered rough-sawn timber slabs—the original cottage floors that, while no longer perfectly aligned, spoke to the home's age and resilience. These boards were in perfect condition, a prime example of construction methods that have stood the test of time. I loved the floors instantly. The only problem was the centimetre-wide gaps that had appeared between each board as they cured over the years. How could we fix that?

One solution was to lift the floor and re-lay it, butting the boards together to remove gaps. It was the optimum fix but beyond our budget, so we opted to fill the gaps with foam tubing, covering it with wood-toned gap filler to give a more seamless appearance. After sanding, I got down on my knees and hand-painted each board with limewash stain, finishing with a flat sheen varnish to seal the floor and create a more authentic, aged look. The process was labour-intensive, but doing it by hand let me control the amount of stain applied, resulting in a more even, natural finish.

The floors now have a patina that's both rustic and refined. Yes, in places it's sagged a little with age, and the paths of those who walked before us have worn dips through the doorways. But therein lies the beauty. There may come a day when we pull up the boards in each room, run them through a mill to remove the uneven colour and lay them again without gaps, but that would be sheer indulgence.

fireplaces in every room

In centuries past, the main heating and cooking source in a home was the fireplace, and Blackbird Cottage was blessed with a functioning chimney in every room. During past renovations, the structures had been covered with plasterboard in an effort to modernise and keep out draughts, but a fireplace in each room was a testament to the warmth and comfort the cottage once provided, even though most were nearly in ruin.

Some would argue that restoring a feature which takes up valuable floor space isn't worth the cost. Indeed, many homeowners remove them—as was done in our cottage's twin next door. But to me, each was an integral part of the cottage's design. There was never a question: they had to be repaired. An old house just doesn't look right when the chimneys are removed. The roofline seems somehow wrong without a chimney, and rooms always feel cosier with a fireplace, even if the fire is never lit.

Restoring the chimneys was no small feat. Once we removed the plaster sheets, the full extent of the damage was revealed, and the bricklayer set to work replacing cracked bricks and repointing the structure with fresh lime mortar. The living room chimney, partly bricked in to accommodate an oil heater, was in the most precarious state. We held our breath as the heater was removed and braces put in place to keep the chimney stable. There was a real concern that the chimney might collapse and bring the roof down too.

But our bricklayer worked his magic, one brick at a time, and in a matter of weeks, Blackbird Cottage had four functional chimneys. We capped them to stop draughts (and birds that kept flying in). Then, I extended the ceiling's creamy hue down the walls to create a lime-washed effect, like the ones I'd admired in cottages on our UK holiday. Now, each chimney feels like part of the room, blending seamlessly with the cottage's palette and bringing a sense of history into our daily lives.

honouring the original roof

According to locals, an Indigenous woman who lived near our cottage in the 1800s was known for crafting roof shingles. She crafted shingles for many of the homes around Port Cygnet during that time, and we believe ours was one of them. While many houses have since been demolished or lost to bushfires, our cottage was luckier. It had survived the elements and a shingle roof was preserved beneath a layer of tin. We felt incredibly fortunate to discover the shingles in such good condition. Seeing them in place after all this time felt like being connected to a piece of our community's history.

While the shingle roof was full of charm and certainly appealed to our love of the old-world, it wasn't practical or sustainable for modern living. And as much as I longed to keep every inch, we installed a galvanised iron roof—one that would endure, yet honour the heritage style so common in Tasmania.

Over a couple of days, each shingle was carefully removed. Those in good condition were set aside to be repurposed as cladding for the new garden shed, allowing their story to continue in a new chapter.

With the roofing task complete, the roof plumber set about crafting custom downpipes to follow the cottage's original lines, lending the home a look that feels timeless rather than trendy. The original cottage had no roof drainage, so it's an update—but one that leans into the past rather than pulling away from it.

For us, restoration was never about removing the puzzle pieces. It was about rearranging them so they could shine again.

LITTLE KEEPSAKE No 12
Shingles uncovered uncovered on the cottage roof. Some perfectly preserved after more than a century. Saved and used in other other projects.

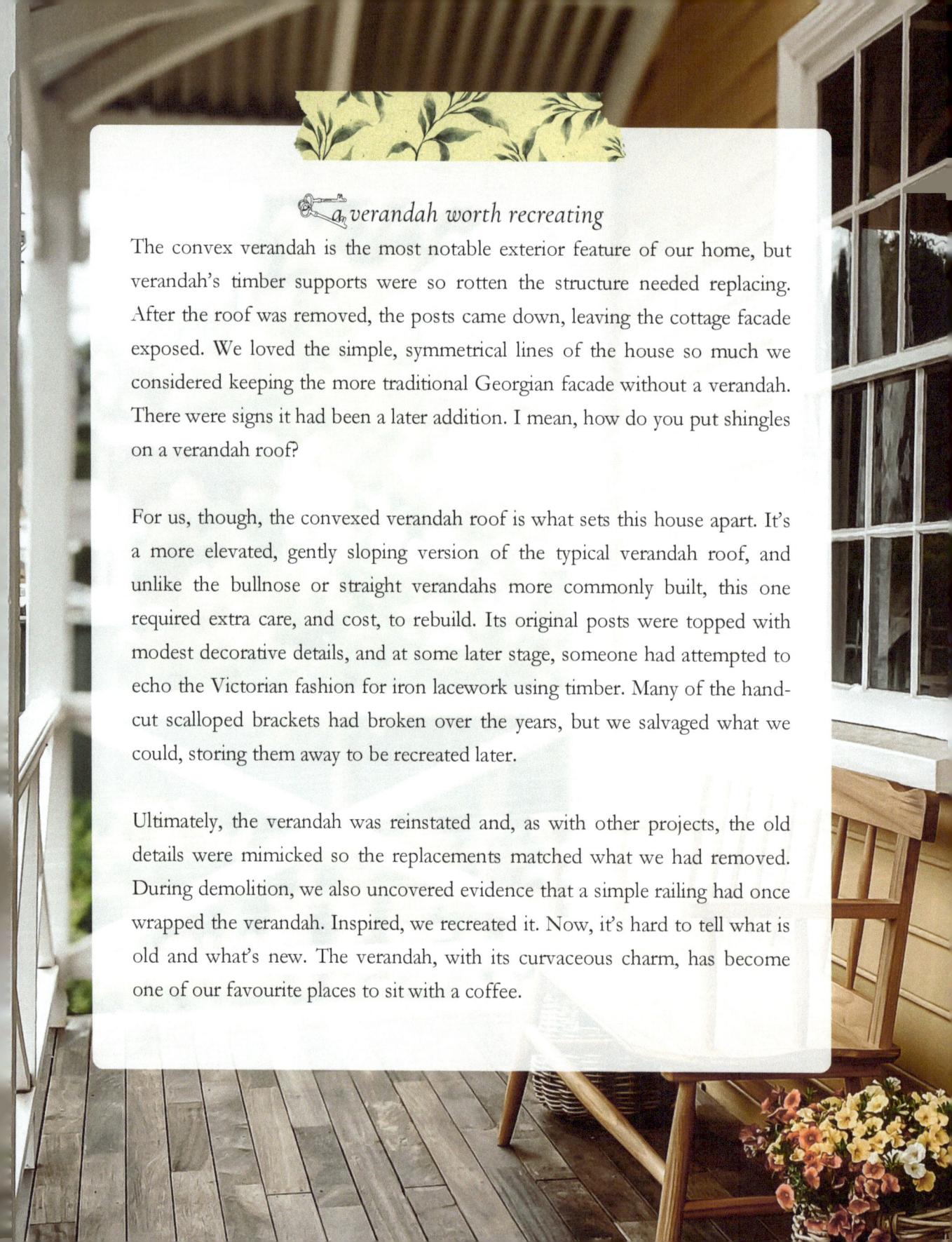

a verandah worth recreating

The convex verandah is the most notable exterior feature of our home, but verandah's timber supports were so rotten the structure needed replacing. After the roof was removed, the posts came down, leaving the cottage facade exposed. We loved the simple, symmetrical lines of the house so much we considered keeping the more traditional Georgian facade without a verandah. There were signs it had been a later addition. I mean, how do you put shingles on a verandah roof?

For us, though, the convexed verandah roof is what sets this house apart. It's a more elevated, gently sloping version of the typical verandah roof, and unlike the bullnose or straight verandahs more commonly built, this one required extra care, and cost, to rebuild. Its original posts were topped with modest decorative details, and at some later stage, someone had attempted to echo the Victorian fashion for iron lacework using timber. Many of the hand-cut scalloped brackets had broken over the years, but we salvaged what we could, storing them away to be recreated later.

Ultimately, the verandah was reinstated and, as with other projects, the old details were mimicked so the replacements matched what we had removed. During demolition, we also uncovered evidence that a simple railing had once wrapped the verandah. Inspired, we recreated it. Now, it's hard to tell what is old and what's new. The verandah, with its curvaceous charm, has become one of our favourite places to sit with a coffee.

the perfect exterior colour

Choosing a colour for the exterior of the cottage wasn't straightforward. Sometimes, colour choices leap out at you, but this wasn't one of those times. We wanted a shade that would honour the past without feeling stuck in it, and we had no intention of choosing from the "heritage palette." I'm fairly sure locals nearly fainted the day we splashed a dozen paint samples along the front of the house. There were plenty of curious glances, and several passers-by didn't hesitate to share their opinions while the swatches lingered on the wall. We were after a showstopper, a colour bold enough to bring the cottage into the new millennium, but **respectful of its roots**. Then, one morning, I climbed the ladder to prime the untouched parts of the facade, and everything changed. As I scraped where old paint met bare timber, a hint of yellow emerged.

It was as if the cottage was revealing another part of her story. I knew from the window restoration that the original trims had been painted a rich, Indian red, and now we had inspiration for the walls, too.

Yellow wasn't a colour I'd thought of for the exterior but, excited, I began searching for a similar shade that would feel fresh, without shouting, "Heritage chic!" from the front gate. After settling on yellow ochre with a modern twist, I knew we'd made the right choice. Custom-tinted to level up the cuteness factor of our cottage, the colour is vibrant, a little cheeky, and the wow factor we wanted.

A scrape of yellow ochre.
A hint of the cottage's past.

A MAP OF BLACKBIRD COTTAGE
a visual guide to cottage life, circa 2025

Office + Bedroom

Master Bedroom

Dining Nook

Freestanding Kitchen

Guest Bedroom

Living Room

Bathroom + Laundry

Drawn from memory and lived experience: the current layout of Blackbird Cottage, as it stands, circa 2025.

Back Garden

Back Porch

OUR STORY IN EVERY ROOM

The memories, meaning, and little decisions
that made this house our home

FIELD NOTES *No 5*

Discovered May 2023

HAND-FORGED NAILS
REMOVED FROM WALL LININGS
HALLWAY | FRONT PARLOUR

This collection of handmade nails held the
cottage together for over a century.
Rough. Imperfect. Beautifully enduring.

OUR STORY IN EVERY ROOM

The memories, meanings and little decisions that made this house a home

Decorating a home is a very personal thing, and it's easy to become lost in the past, wondering who lived in a home or how each room was once used. What can make a home truly special is the way we weave our story into that history, layering it with our journey, our loves, and our memories. In doing so, we don't overwrite what came before; we become part of the history of the house.

As I began the process of developing the interior scheme for the cottage, I realised every choice I made would also be a conversation with the past. I didn't want to impose a design on the cottage; I wanted to uncover the soul already within it, then bring that into the new century. Each room became its own chapter, an individual expression of the history of the house, while keeping to my overall scheme and colour palette.

Some choices, like the heritage replica floral wallpaper, or the gingham seat pads in the kitchen, were my way of weaving in the warmth and nostalgia I longed for. Through layers of texture, colour and handpicked objects, I aimed to create a space that felt as though it had evolved naturally over the years, rather than being designed all at once.

This section of the book is a walk through each space, sharing the choices I made, the moments that shaped them, and the design philosophy that guided me. Blackbird Cottage isn't just a collection of rooms. It's a home with a heart, a place where every corner tells a story.

A PASSAGE REIMAGINED
from thoroughfare to feature

Above the new light switch is where I first spotted the wallpaper that shaped the entire renovation.

BEFORE

Dingy and unloved, the hallway was a pass-through to the living room. Torn wallpaper, threadbare carpet, and a sea of stains.

AFTER

Now it's a welcoming passage filled with character. The design and styling make it feel more like a room than a route.

"Even a hallway deserves its moment: a bit of boldness, some texture, and a plan for what it could become."

Entry Hall
MOOD BOARD

Milk glass pendant to echo the original

COLOURS

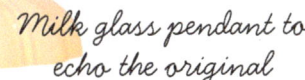

new door hardware

art by Richard Stanley

chair rail detail

inspired by nature

neutral hall runner

THE WELCOME WE WALK THROUGH
A narrow hall, a broad invitation

THE DISCOVERY BEHIND THE ELECTRICITY BOX. LAYER ON LAYER OF WALLPAPER

For five years, I had a grand hallway. two metres wide and nearly nine metres long. It was vast, echoey and elegant, but in its own way, just as tricky to decorate as any small space. I eventually learned to let that hall breathe: rugs and artwork were all it needed.

Blackbird Cottage, as ever, presented a new kind of challenge, one I hadn't worked with since The Colourful House in Perth. A dark, narrow hall. A hall that, at barely a metre wide and just under four metres long, makes bringing larger pieces into the house feel like you're part of a human Tetris puzzle and requires the flexibility of a yoga professional. The hall is not a gathering space, but it is the first space our guests step into, and so, the look I designed had to begin at the door. Like the rest of the cottage, the hall was in a sad state. The interior hadn't been touched in decades. Previous owners, who'd purchased with plans to renovate, had begun the process of stripping the house back to its bones. Wallpaper peeled from the walls, linoleum cracked and curled where carpet had once been, and a dirty glass pendant light hung from the centre of the ceiling. The front door was secured with a makeshift barrel bolt, only fit for a shed. The keeper of the original lock was long gone. Still, the space had potential. The challenge was in harnessing and releasing it.

It was a discovery behind the old electricity junction box that helped the design decisions along. The box, relocated many years before, had been mounted on a piece of cement sheet. This remained and been papered over. But, behind it, was a 30cm square of wallpaper, hidden since the 1920s. Its delicate Art Nouveau pattern, in soft shades of green, was an exciting find. We were uncovering a historical time capsule.

As we peeled the paper back, more layers revealed themselves, each a remnant of someone else's taste and time. In that unexpected moment, I was certain the house was showing us the direction we needed to take. That small fragment of pattern and palette became the starting point for the entire house. We hadn't planned to follow the past so closely, but Blackbird Cottage had other ideas.

creating the look

A milk glass pendant: A nod to the shade that was there

With the bones of the hallway revealed and preparation done, I could shift focus from renovation to decoration, the part I love most. I'd made the bold choice, but I'll admit, seeing my colour choices on a wall for the first time was both exciting and nerve-wracking. I was apprehensive that choosing darker tones might make the narrow space feel more closed in, rather than creating the intimacy I was hoping for.

Another problem I faced when designing the look for the hall was how to add interest to the walls without physically encroaching into the space.

It was clear that no furniture could be added, so a gorgeous runner and artwork would have to feature prominently.

My first task was to install architrave and corner blocks to the doors, a simple job that transformed the hall from plain to pretty. Then I used paint to mimic the effect of a chair rail one third of the way up the wall, painting the lower portion in green, and drenching the top two-thirds and ceiling with cream. The effect was dramatic, but still lacking. I contemplated ways to add even more interest in the form of wallpaper, beadboard, or the regency panelling we planned for the kitchen. In the end, I chose restraint, installing simple wainscoting below the timber chair rail I'd added. The wainscot adds the perfect amount of dimension and depth without overwhelming the narrow hall.

A neutral hall runner. Not overpowering the hall

Carrying the green paint down over the skirting boards to the floor helped elongate the space and gave the illusion of higher walls, too. Above, the warm white kept things light, bouncing the natural light that filtered through the space. It began to feel cohesive and timeless.

accessories for the space

Lighting in a hallway isn't just practical—it's atmospheric. In a small space, a single fixture can become the focal point. A scalloped milk glass pendant felt just right: sweet, subtle, and reminiscent of the light that once hung there. The touch of brass ties in with the fittings elsewhere in the cottage, adding just enough warmth and shine. Its soft curves echo motifs found throughout the house and bring a warm gleam to the shadows.

A hallway runner is one of my favourite ways to add texture and interest without crowding the floor. A neutral, patterned rug now stretches the length of the space but doesn't compete with the wall colours or artwork. It's more modern, follows the natural progression down the hall, and can be swapped when my mood, or the season, changes. Gavin and I are drawn to unique art, too, not just antiques or vintage finds, but pieces that speak to us in a personal way. We'd already collected a series of works by a local artist and had them framed in simple oak.

The scenes are drawn from the landscape surrounding the cottage and, thus, spark conversation when guests wander through the house, as they so often do. Lined along the hall, they offer interest without overwhelming the narrow space and make the hall feel considered, not crowded.

Even if your hallway allows only a sliver of wall space, the ideas opposite might spark your imagination—and remind you that a hall can be more than just a passage.

In the end, a hallway, no matter how narrow, is more than a walkway. It's the first glimpse of your home. It should feel like an invitation to stay awhile.

MINI FEATURE No 7

LITTLE HALLWAY MOMENTS
that turn a pass through space into a hello

- A peg or hook rail
- A hanging plant or potted fern
- A row of antique hooks on a shelf above the door
- A built in wall niche
- Framed vintage postcards or dried botanicals
- A shallow cabinet for shoes.
- A wall sconce or candle shelf
- Painted chair or picture rail
- Wallpaper above or below panelling
- A statement light fixture

A SPACE REKINDLED
from crumbling brick to the soul of the cottage

Every home has a heart. This restoration is where the heart of the cottage began to beat again.

BEFORE

Once the cottage kitchen, this room was dark and cold. It bore the marks of more than one renovation.

AFTER

Now it's a cosy space at the centre of the home with restored brick work, oodles of light, and thoughtful touches.

"Removed the heater. Held our breath. Ceiling stayed. Miracles do happen."

Living Room
MOOD BOARD

wire chandelier

COLOURS

pattern on pattern

reupholstered chair

chair rail detail

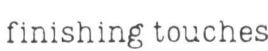

finishing touches

inspired by nature

A Room Created for Relaxing
Designing a Cosy Living Space in a Small Area

BLOCK PRINT DRAPES | A WELL-TRAVELLED CUPBOARD

If the kitchen is the heart of the home, the living room is its soul. Cottage life naturally leans towards cosy, but lean too far and it can quickly tip into cluttered, especially when you start layering on comfort.

Anyone who has visited my home or sat in one of my classrooms knows I don't like clutter. I can't function when every horizontal surface is filled. I love a decorated space, but shelves must feel organised, with intentional displays rather than haphazard. In our cottage, everything needs a place and a purpose. The living room is no different.

Creating the look

After downsizing from our large farmhouse, and its equally large furniture, designing a living room less than two-thirds the size became a creative challenge. At the farm, we'd enjoyed an expansive open-plan space, with a snug for movie watching. Now, all those functions had to fit within one small room: cosy nights of TV, quiet reading, small gatherings, and the occasional glass of wine. I had the benefit of original architecture in a charming cottage window, restored chimney, and beautiful board and batten ceiling, but the room needed to seat five or six, accommodate a TV, offer storage, and include occasional tables.

There needed to be places for lighting and horizontal surfaces to display collected items, vases and books. A tall order for a space under four metres wide.

With the colour scheme decided, my focus turned to the furniture and the story it would tell. My favourite pieces from Green Gate Farm were waiting in storage. I already had armchairs, side tables, and stools, but because I love a space that feels cosy and slightly unexpected, I chose to mix antiques with a modern, boxy sofa and a rattan rug. This balance between old and new brings comfort without formality, character without clutter.

Infusing character

Located at the heart of the cottage, the living room connects most of the house and can be seen from several rooms, including the front door. Because the bedroom, kitchen and hallway are all visible, the colours needed to flow seamlessly. To do this, I continued my colour theme and style from the front hall to the living room, painting the upper walls in C.R.E.A.M., paired with Wild Thing, that moody olive green below the chair rail. The darker tone grounds the space with both character and practicality. Together, these colours create structure without formality and warmth without heaviness. They ensure that my cohesive palette can carry from room to room.

Mixing old with new is key to ensuring the space feels fresh while honouring the historic charm I love. The IKEA sofa, covered in a deep mustard corduroy slipcover from Norse Maison, adds warmth and texture. Golden accents catch the light and bounce it around the room, creating a softness that pairs beautifully with the aged timber and vintage touches. This cover, a deliberate choice, connects the living space to the yellow shade of the master bedroom wallpaper. It's made from washable cotton, an essential for dog life, and easily changeable for future updates.

LITTLE KEEPSAKE No 13
A fragile clipping of local men mid-match, found beneath the carpet underlay. Folded and forgotten, yet never quite lost. Their cheers still echo through the floorboards. A playful legacy beneath our feet.

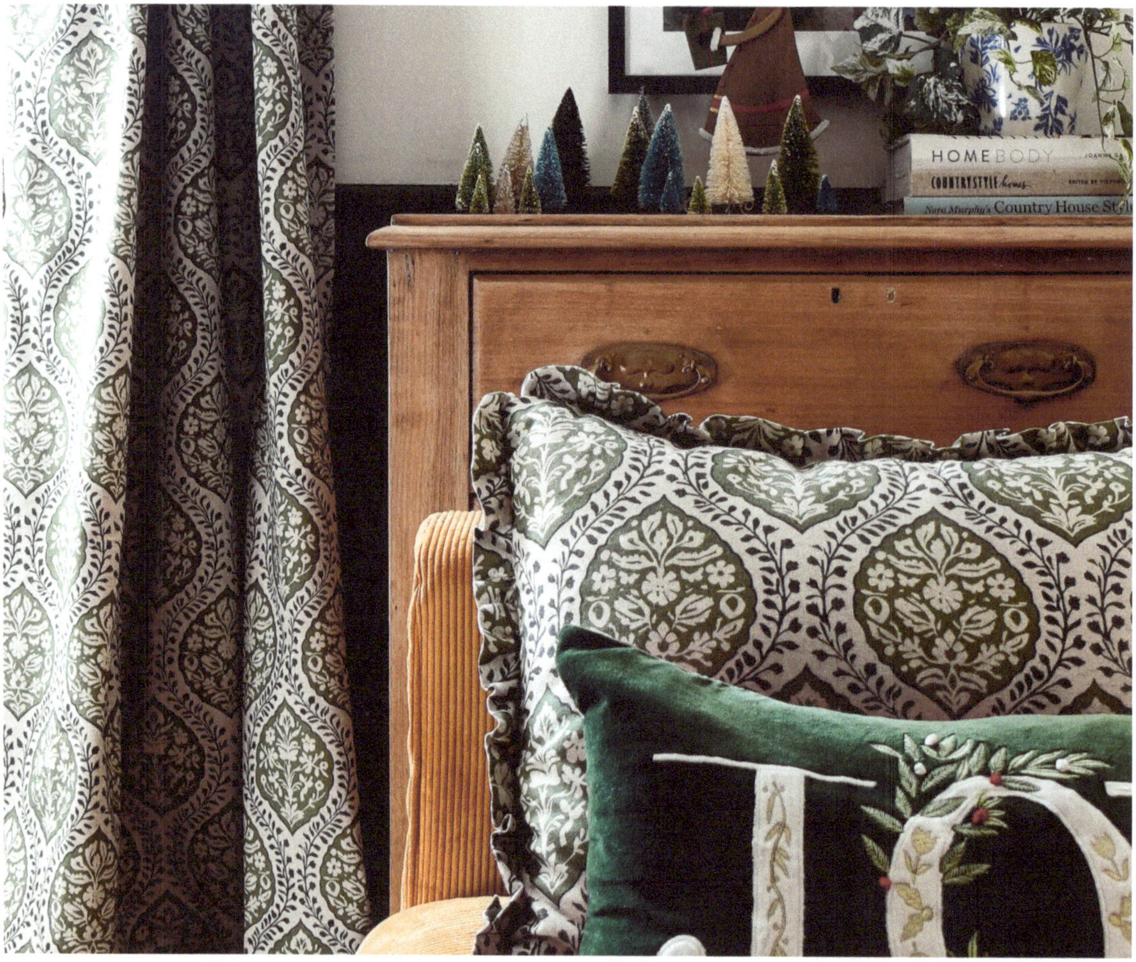
HOMEBODY
COUNTRYSTYLE homes
Nora Murphy's Country House

LONDON

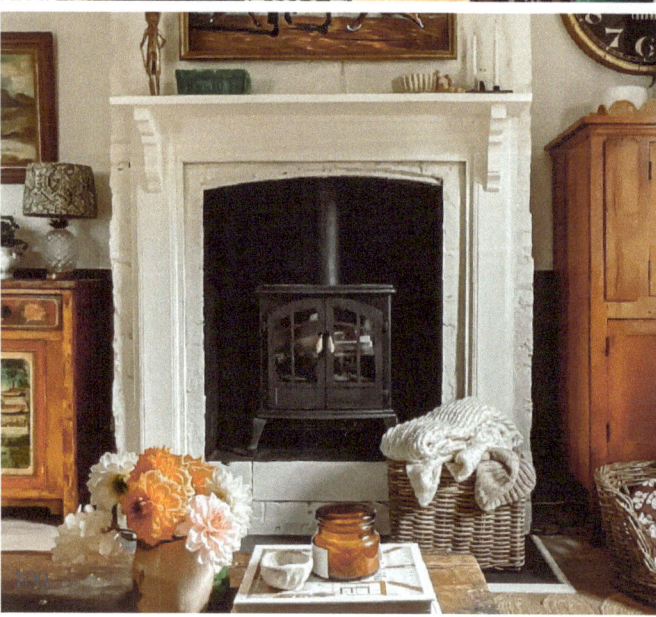

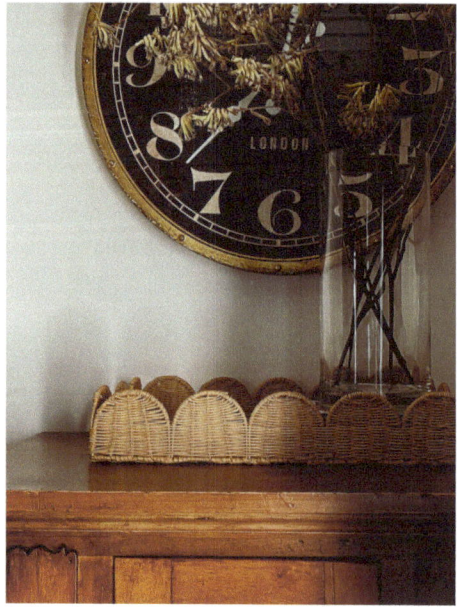

The antique armchairs, with their generous curves and carved detail, flank the sofa, contrasting its modern simplicity with charm. For now, they're painted with leftover wall paint that's been softened with fabric softener. At some stage, I'll reupholster them in cream linen.

Heating is vital, not only in Tasmania, but especially in the cottage. Even with insulation old houses can be cold. After installing Thermosoft radiators throughout, the living room still lacked cosy and I knew it was flames we were missing. The fireplace had no fire. To solve the problem, we purchased an electric fire to fit in the chimney space. Now, when we feel the need for the cosy comfort of a fire, we turn it on with the flame effect only.

Nothing's matchy-matchy in this room. Every item was chosen for its scale, shape, and beauty. Some were auction finds for less than twenty dollars; others cost far more. But each thing brings texture and softness, creating a layered, lived-in feel.

The cottage look in decor

When the living room was first primed white and ready for paint, it felt clean and pleasant, yet lacked depth. I was determined to keep the light-filled feeling we'd created, but I wanted warmth and definition too, so the layers I added needed to honour that brightness while deepening the mood.

Accessories create character without clutter. In cooler months, woollen tartan throws in navy and green are draped over the sofa, adding texture and comfort. These practical souvenirs from our Scotland trip are as useful as they are decorative.

The linen panel curtains, made from an Etsy-sourced block-printed fabric, add depth without fuss. Their modern, almost graphic scroll design feels like a contemporary take on heritage style and a nod to Victorian without tipping into chintz.

In true Laura Ashley fashion, I couldn't resist making matching cushions and a pleated lampshade from the leftover fabric. These small details tie the space together, while reinforcing the cottage's tactile, layered aesthetic. Antique brass curtain rods and clips are used throughout the house to complete the look and keep sightlines visually cohesive.

Cushions shift with the seasons. Right now, the sofa is dressed in block-printed covers with tiny ruffles and ribbon ties. As the year progresses, these are swapped for ginghams, florals, or stripes in gold, green, cream, or burgundy. Cushions are my quick way to change a mood: stacked in abundance or reduced to a single pillow, depending on the season. Those not in use are stored in vacuum-sealed bags inside the pine corner cupboard.

My accessories reflect what I love: auction finds, family heirlooms, handmade treasures. Our coffee table, an 1800s trunk, is scuffed and worn from years of socked feet resting on its edges. On its dark surface, I style simple vignettes like decorating books, a bowl, fresh flowers, or a candle. These are moved when space is needed for board games or drinks.

Artwork personalises the room further. Above the sofa hangs 'Tulloch', a folk-style painting we grabbed at auction for ninety dollars. I've never been a horse person, but the style, colours, and proportions just worked. Happily, the green in the grass echoes the lower wall colour, making it feel intentional.

In the opposite corner, a pair of 1960s George Hughes prints layer blues into the palette, complementing the walls and turning the corner into a charming vignette.

MINI FEATURE No 8

COTTAGE FINDS TO TELL A STORY

Touches to bring warmth to a home

- Scalloped trims
- Gilt inlays and aged brass accents
- Auction finds under $50
- Heirloom pieces
- Reupholstered vintage chairs
- Handmade or collected oil paintings
- Rustic trunks as coffee tables
- Mismatched, well-loved furniture

For me, accessories and art are about creating warmth and telling a story. Whether it's old paintings or original art purchased on a trip, it's the colours and subjects that matter most, not whether a piece is technically 'right'.

And what about the TV? I wasn't willing to let a black screen dominate the living room. The solution was a Samsung Frame TV, mounted above the chimney breast. We created a custom frame from leftover chair rail and painted it antique gold. Now, when the TV is switched off, it becomes a digital artwork. I can change the image seasonally, making the TV a decorative feature rather than an eyesore.

the icing on the cake

Lighting is the icing on the design cake, a final flourish that ties everything together. In the evenings, lighting transforms the living room. Mismatched lamps, many with shades covered in leftover fabrics, cast pools of light in dark corners. A rechargeable lamp covered in pleated gingham sits atop the mantel. The lack of cords give flexibility, and the warm glow invites relaxation. My favourite lamp, a pineapple-style knockoff, has been upgraded with gold paint and a pleated shade. A low-hung pendant was something I was determined to have in our living room. Without the option for hardwiring, I turned to a three metre plug-in cord, which I hung in the corner of the room. It's practical, removable, and the tiny frilled glass shade adds dimension and whimsy, especially when lit in the evenings. We have overhead lighting too, in the form of a wire chandelier. With small wicker shades echoing other pendants in the house, it softens light and provides visual continuity. Like most ceiling fixtures in the cottage, it's on a dimmer, but we rarely switch it on.

This room will always be a work in progress. Layers will be added, pieces swapped, but at this moment, the living room tells a story of comfort, history, and elegance. Sunlight casts golden strokes across the floorboards, and the honeyed corduroy of the sofa invites you to curl up with a book or lounge over a movie. Objects collected over years settle naturally here, like they've always belonged. They've earned their place in our home.

A ROOM REBUILT
anchored in the past, created for today

Since we couldn't make the kitchen bigger, we gave it better views, inserting as many windows as we could reasonably justify.

BEFORE

A dated lean-to with patchwork flooring and makeshift plumbing. No flow, no light, and absolutely no charm.

AFTER

Now the working heart of the home, this space balances vintage charm with everyday practicality.

"The day the builders asked how I planned to fit a sink into an antique cabinet was the day I learned deep breathing wasn't just for yoga."

Kitchen
MOOD BOARD

natural textures

COLOURS

table 'island' bench'

flagstone-look floor

wall panelling + pegrails

mixed metal accents

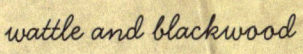

wattle and blackwood

History Returns to the Kitchen
A new kitchen made from old pieces

A MIX OF ANTIQUE PINE MODERNISED WITH STONE WORKTOPS

The kitchen loomed large as both a challenge and a possibility in the renovation. The structure we inherited was not up to code, and the costs to rebuild were high, so our thoughts alternated between knocking it down or somehow renovating within the walls.

Eventually, we decided to demolish and use the moment to create something unique. The challenge was to build a room that made the most of the remaining renovation budget while not going over it, a room that was filled with warmth, texture, and a sense of history.

The kitchen design began with the huge pine dresser we brought with us from Green Gate Farm. We'd bought it as an anniversary gift to ourselves a few years previously, so there was no question it was going to be part of the kitchen design. Despite the draftsman trying to talk me into other layouts, I was determined to have two expanses of empty wall specifically to house that dresser. That way I could pick the space best suited when the time came. In many ways, the dresser anchored everything visually, emotionally and practically. It was from that starting point, the kitchen concept grew in layers, as all good spaces should.

My original mood board featured pieces both aspirational and practical: a deep ceramic sink, an antique bronze bridge faucet, and scalloped brass wall scones I'd found online. At first, I imagined cabinetry in a rich green, paired with creamy retro appliances and copper hardware. But as budget reality set in, and our building plans were trimmed to satisfy council requirements, my vision had to change. I simply wasn't prepared to spend a massive chunk of our remaining cash on generic cabinetry we'd have to install and paint ourselves.

And so, our European-style cottage kitchen came to life. It wasn't from a showroom, but from a patchwork of antique finds, clever rethinks, and a fair bit of painter's tape stuck on the floor.

Building the history in

Like so many elements of a renovation, our final choices were shaped not just by aesthetics but by practicality. We had a desire to tread lightly, both financially and environmentally. With the builders on-site and trades needing to know the appliance positions, the pressure was on to design a kitchen that felt as though it had always been there, and have it ready to install in a matter of weeks. Why? Because me being me, I'd booked us a holiday to the UK. We had a housesitter arriving to look after Bonnie. A functioning kitchen and bathroom was essential.

We began collecting antique hutches and sideboards from all over the state, pieces chosen for their scale, patina, and adaptability. Some were Marketplace finds; others were quality antiques from the kind of store I'd once only dreamed of buying from. A French pine cabinet with tiny drawers became our pantry. A handsome English buffet offered the perfect counter depth beside the sink area. Two kauri hutches were reimagined. The first cradling the sink and the other forming a prep area beside the oven. The upper portions of those hutches were set aside for future use elsewhere in the home. Decisions such as these, to salvage and reuse rather than throw away, are made with the design in mind. They're not born of the need to balance the budget on every occasion, but to create a look that feels in keeping with the house.

MINI FEATURE No 9

PIECES WORTH THE HUNT
Treasures that bring a touch of whimsy

- Antique pine hutches & sideboards
- Plate racks
- Tiny shelf units
- Cabinets with tongue-and-groove or scalloped details
- Vintage tables that can be reused as an island
- Large laundry or linen style cabinets that can be used for storage
- Wicker anything
- Metal canisters
- A set of vintage scales with weights
- Old breadboards and vintage jars

Each piece arrived with its own story: where we found it, who we met, who built it. Those little stories now live on in our kitchen, giving the room a resonance that no new build could replicate.

To visually unify the varying heights and depths of our freestanding pieces, we built out the backs where needed with framing timber, then added a timber shadow line beneath the work surface, this subtly elevated the antique cabinets to modern working height. A creamy stone benchtop was installed across the length, creating a continuous surface and a polished contrast to the warmth of the pine. The benchtop ties the pieces together and protects the pieces from everyday bumps. If we ever decide to change the kitchen, the pine buffet can be removed and repurposed elsewhere. Above the range, we clad the hood in salvaged timber from the tops of the hutches used as base cabinets and finished it with original decorative moulding. Open shelves were made from framing pine to create a chunky look, then stained with coffee and sealed with a matte finish. Cast iron brackets strike a utilitarian note.

The integrated dishwasher, a purchase before we committed to a freestanding layout, was concealed inside a custom pine cabinet built from inexpensive timber. I stained it to match the other pieces, then added antique brass and porcelain pulls to keep the look cohesive, and convincing. The cabinet blends seamlessly into the space, and the intentionally mismatched handles only enhance the room's collected, lived-in charm.

AN OLD WORLD FEEL WITH MODERN DAY FUNCTIONALITY

lighting sets the mood

One of the joys of renovating is finding that sweet spot where vision and budget align. In the past, I've often swapped out light fittings rather than rewire an entire room but, in the cottage kitchen, I finally got to indulge my design instincts.

With a loose layout in mind, I set about creating a lighting plan that would do more than just illuminate the space. It needed to layer task and ambient lighting thoughtfully, yet still leave room for charm.

I avoid downlights wherever possible, but this kitchen has a lower ceiling than the rest of the cottage, meaning too many pendants would look busy. So, we planned a series of downlights for task lighting, blending them with the ceiling colour, then added statement lighting to create the room's old-world feel. Brass pleated sconces were installed on either side of the range to bring a little sparkle and a rattan table lamp sits beside the coffee machine, perfect for those early morning winter brews. I've popped it on a timer, so it's ready to light the way on dark mornings.

The look is finished off with reproduction light switches from my favourite heritage hardware company, TradCo. When the cottage was first built, there was no electricity, so these switches feel like the perfect old-world compromise. It's small details like this that evoke a sense of history, without ever shouting "fake."

finishing touches

This is a kitchen that was never meant to be static. It was designed to evolve year by year. It's meant to be layered with meaningful pieces, seasonal touches, and sentimental favourites. One of my most treasured elements is the plate rack Gavin built, printed with my grandmother's scone recipe. It's both a conversation starter and a place to display mismatched china that changes with the seasons: tulip cups in spring, rare Meakin sandwich plates in autumn, a cheerful collection of Christmas mugs in December.

I love layering the everyday with the unexpected: a stack of plates in front of a vintage print, an old French decoy duck perched on the windowsill, or a pair of wooden skittles that serve no purpose but to amuse me with their odd charm.

Gavin's table, crafted from antique French cheese boards and repurposed table legs, became a working island and one of the most practical changes we made. Once a dumping ground, it's now our main prep space, allowing us to cook while facing guests and joining the conversation. Baskets tucked beneath it store oversized items that don't fit in the pantry. These lived-in layers keep the kitchen feeling natural, rather than styled or staged.

In a cottage kitchen, fittings matter just as much as furniture. We chose a farmhouse sink that's deep enough to soak oven trays and generous enough to hold an armful of garden flowers. Paired with an antique bronze faucet, it brings a sense of tradition to the space and has become my favourite place to stand and watch the view.

Near the back door, we added a peg rail to create a makeshift mudroom. It's where coats and hats land after morning walks with the dogs, and baskets hang within easy reach. Near the pantry door, a set of hooks holds chopping boards and bread paddles. These small design choices, often decided mid-build, are the ones that bring romance to everyday life.

ESSENTIALS FOR A COTTAGE KITCHEN
a practical list for heartfelt style

FOR FUNCTION + CHARM
- Freestanding furniture
- Farmhouse/ceramic sink
- Brass or bronze tapware
- Natural stone or stone-look tiles
- Decorative timber details
- Hooks, hook & more hooks

LAYERED STORAGE
- woven baskets
- vintage jars
- repurposed containers
- peg rails and hooks

COTTAGE FIXTURES
- Open shelving
- Reproduction switches and traditional fixtures
- Vintage-style lighting

Cost-Conscious Creativity

The kitchen, including the antique furniture, sink, tapware and, lighting came in at a fraction of the cost quoted for a basic flat pack kitchen install.

By doing our research and sourcing thoughtfully, we created a kitchen that feels entirely ours. It reflects our style as much as our values: resourcefulness, individuality, and a love of good design with a story to tell.

STYLING TOUCHES
for a homely, welcoming feel

fresh flowers

seasonal china

a twig wreath

candles

linen tea towels

- Fresh flowers or garden cuttings
- A cloche filled with cookies or cakes
- A stack of teacups or plates ready to use
- Seasonal china
- Linen tea towels and table runners
- Twig wreath with long, wispy ribbons
- Candles and warm lamps
- A rug by the sink for cold mornings
- Crock for utensils
- Trays for soaps and oils
- Shelf vignettes with framed prints, postcards, or signs
- A ceramic bowl of seasonal fruit
- Collected trinkets with a tale
- Vintage cake stands and tins

a gathered collection of simple items to make a house feel like home

A CORNER TRANSFORMED
from forgotten lean-to to sunlit sanctuary

"This wall held a niche that once peeked into the kitchen. It was home to dusty jars and questionable boxes we didn't dare open."

BEFORE

Dirty, cramped and barely functional, this lean-to laundry had a view that deserved to be revealed.

AFTER

Now it's the most loved corner of the cottage. A room with a view, created for living and entertaining.

"Good things take time, great things take woman with a vision and a man with a hammer and the patience of a saint."

Dining Nook
MOOD BOARD

oversize scallop pendant to echo those in bedrooms

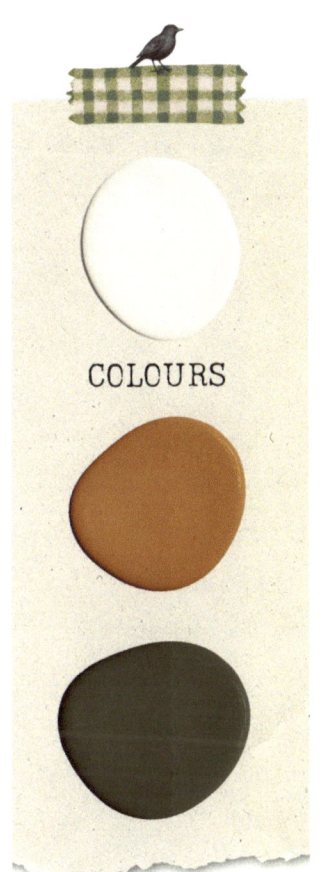

COLOURS

mix of chairs + bench seating

original kitchen wallpaper

linen cafe curtains

seasonal styling

wattle and blackwood

MEALS SHARED, MEMORIES MADE
A dining nook where family and friends gather

BUILT FOR LINGERING | A LITTLE NOOK WITH A BIG JOB

From the earliest design sketches of Blackbird Cottage's kitchen there was one feature I refused to let go of: the dining nook. I pictured it clearly—guests nestled into cushions, coffee in hand, bathed in afternoon light as the water shimmered just beyond the window. No matter what changes had to be made elsewhere in the design plan, the nook remained. In a room that would function as a kitchen, dining area, and hosting space, the nook was a non-negotiable.

Originally, I imagined the bench wrapping around a large circular table, creating an intimate corner for long lunches and late-night chats. My vision was for guests to be wowed by the view as they sat at the table, and in that, we pulled it off. However, the final iteration came with a few compromises. In hindsight, I should have thought more carefully about the ramifications of a corner nook hemmed in by cabinetry on both sides. It makes getting in and out a slightly clunky affair. But the bigger issue, for me, is the bench height. And I write this so you might learn from my mistake. My intention was to build the bench a little below the standard 45cm height, knowing I'd be adding a plush, comfy cushion on top. But Gavin (and our carpenter), both on the taller side, were convinced it should be 50cm. I relented, and now my feet barely graze the floor. Tiny footstools tucked beneath the bench have since saved the day.

The shape of the nook presented challenges too. One side butts up against the kitchen cabinetry, the other is slightly impeded by the cabinet. This limited our choice of table, and meant the planned table did not sit comfortably in the space. Eventually, fate stepped in. At an auction, we stumbled across an antique circular pine table, and it turned out to be a perfect fit. The original rectangular table, our second choice for the nook, now serves as our kitchen island.

a playful palette

The decoration of this little space was the easiest part. I leaned into softness and texture to soften the kitchen's practical finished, deliberately choosing brighter greens and blues to echo the garden outside, knowing the natural light would soften everything further. After a failed attempt to reproduce the wallpaper pattern found on the living room wall as fabric, I stumbled across a roll of hydrangea-print linen that felt like it had been waiting for me. Paired with Japanese cottons in varying shades of green and blue, plus my favourite gingham in a more vibrant tone, the fabric created a relaxed palette that defines the corner. One day, I'll create that wallpaper-inspired fabric. It would bring a pop of heritage charm to this nook.

layout option

vintage table

linen curtains

Everything is designed to be interchangeable: cushion covers swapped with the seasons, the blues packed away in favour of browns and olives during cooler months. The seat cushion is simply foam cut to size and wrapped in an inexpensive cotton that can be removed or replaced. (A friend suggested red and white for Christmas, so tempting!)

A scalloped rattan pendant hangs above the table, custom-made to match the bedroom fittings and add visual warmth. In the evenings, it's dimmed to create a cosy dining effect. It's a perfect match for the set of rattan chairs I purchased. Their arched tops and textured backs bring a modern element into the room.

small space hosting

Hosting in a small space has meant leaning into flexibility. Our round table comfortably seats four or five on a typical day, but one of the biggest adjustments to downsizing, and cottage life in general, was finding a new way to entertain.

The cottage kitchen is perfect for a stand-up drinks party, but full sit-down gatherings required some creative thinking. At one point, we used the kitchen island as a table, pulling up chairs when needed. It worked in theory but never truly felt right because, when not in use, it felt like we had a rogue table floating in the middle of the room. Another attempt saw us bringing in a long table from outdoors and setting it diagonally from the nook with added chairs. Again, charming in theory but impractical in practice. I even flirted with the idea of adding bar stools to the island and having everyone perch there. The struggle was real.

But for now, we've found our way. The island becomes a buffet station when space is tight, The small table is removed, creating a seating area in the nook, while a trestle is set up in front of the cabinet. Our nook chairs are used at the table and extras brought in from the shed. Again, not a perfect solution, but a solution. And, once the table is set, it looks pretty and is narrow enough for guest to move around.

The nook has become more than just a place to eat. It's where days begin slowly and friends linger long after the meal is done. It's a space that reminds us, over and over, why we chose this little cottage in the first place: not just for beauty, but for moments like these.

A FLORAL RETREAT
from bare boards to a room in full flower

We found old newspaper clippings, ads for corsets and frocks, little reminders of women who'd once lived here.

BEFORE

Stripped back to its bones, this room had charm buried, but it took imagination to see it could be something special.

AFTER

Now it's a warm and welcoming retreat, wrapped in floral wallpaper, a space to dream of new projects.

"The wallpaper we chose was floral, but the one we uncovered was wilder, with daisies trailing over the wall like they owned the place."

A PLACE FOR SLEEPING & DREAMING
Bedrooms with old soul charm

PATTERNED WALLS | VINTAGE FIBRES | DAPPLED LIGHT

Creating a restful bedroom is a priority, yet in many homes we've lived in, it's the last room to be finished. We focus on the spaces visitors will see, and then, inevitably, the money or energy runs out —and the bedroom stays unfinished. It's odd, really, when you consider how much time we spend there.

At Blackbird Cottage, I was determined not to fall into that trap. I've spent too many years in bedrooms that were half-finished or lacking in warmth and charm. This house deserved better and so did we. A bedroom should feel like a retreat, an escape from the world.

For me, the foundation of a restful bedroom isn't about what you add, it's about what you take away. In a world filled with noise, screens and endless to-do lists, the bedroom should be a sanctuary. No harsh lighting. No piles of paperwork. No visual reminders of work left undone. I focus on a few simple things that bring me calm: natural fibres, vintage pieces, and a pile of books beside my bed. Layered textiles, dappled light through sheer lace panels, and simple furniture are what gave the Victorian cottage bedroom its warmth. That sense of comfort and history was exactly what I wanted to capture at Blackbird Cottage.

The bedroom is an opportunity to use textiles to create a big transformation with minimal effort. The Victorians understood the power of drapes, soft rugs underfoot, and cotton sheets worn smooth with use. I follow their lead, layering a mix of quilts, washed linen, and crisp cotton. In winter, I bring out wool blankets and flannelette sheets. In summer, I switch to fabrics that feel lighter visually and physically.

Furniture doesn't need to match. In fact, mismatched pieces often create a more restful room than one styled like a showroom. An old chest of drawers, a preloved bedside table and, an antique bed frame can create charm without trying. Personal touches like a family photo, a posy of garden flowers in a small vase, or a little dish for jewellery then complete the story.

the main bedroom

After filling a shoebox with wallpaper samples, I finally chose Nocturne by Borastapeter for the master bedroom. Its deep ochre tone brings immediate warmth to this small room on the western side of the cottage, while its subtle floral pattern, with delicate rose-gold centres, nods to the original wallpapers we discovered during renovation. Borastapeter's reimagined vintage prints suit the old-world bones of the cottage, yet feel timeless with a modern twist.

The furnishings take second place here, to allow the wallpaper to shine. We've replaced the interim wardrobes with custom-built cabinetry, designed to echo traditional cottage cupboards. Painted to match the chimney breast and fitted with understated knobs that mirror the window hardware, they offer ample storage while blending into the architecture of the room. The addition allowed us to remove the chest of drawers, creating breathing room.

A pair of nightstands, purchased for sixty dollars and painted a soft yellow, flank our large iron bed. The nightstands are deliberately simple in shape; their barley twist detail a heritage nod. For now, they're a pretty addition that serves a practical purpose. Styled with plants and a trinket bowl, there is plenty of space for books and a morning coffee.

To warm the floor, a large Persian-style rug from the attic bedroom at Green Gate Farm anchors the space. Its burgundy and gold tones complement the ochre walls, adding depth and grounding the room. Though almost wall-to-wall, the rug leaves glimpses of timber visible—an intentional choice to preserve a sense of history.

Layers on layers

The bed in our room is dressed with plain linen duvet covers, mixed with ruffled or patterned pillows and gingham quilts for seasonal change. My preference is for quality linen for longevity, coordinated with less expensive cotton items that are replaced to match the time of year: autumn toned gingham, a forest green waffle duvet, a block print quilt or a chunky knit throw in a deep rust.

Dressing the bed is a quick affair, now I'm opting for a long bolster cushion, rather than a mountain of cushions we do not use and have no room to store. The bolster gives the bed a finished look while retaining an air of simplicity.

Custom built robes to mimic the look of heritage cabinets

A persian rug keeps our feet warm on cold mornings

But bedding isn't the only source of interest in our room. Layering in other elements, using the Red Thread from other rooms keeps the scheme cohesive.

Wall sconces in rattan chosen particularly for their warm tones and delicate swing arms in brass, frame the bed. A scalloped rattan pendant shade, a detail echoed elsewhere in the house, continues the playful tone and the mixing of old with new. Cream linen curtain panels hang from dainty brass rods, also drawing on the curtain look in other rooms. To block the morning light without adding visual weight, inexpensive cotton sheets are clipped behind them, creating a billowy effect.

A whimsical light fitting carries rattan into the bedroom

Every piece in this room has been chosen for function as much as beauty. Storage baskets, under-bed totes, and the small faux bamboo drawers tucked into the old fireplace all serve a purpose. The addition of a new mantel, to replace one removed decades ago, was carefully planned so the wardrobes on either side still function properly. The mantel has added dimension to a wall that was in danger of looking flat after the sides were filled in. Now, I have a small area for displaying bedroom appropriate decor, and even better… Christmas decorating.

BEAUTY IN THE DARKEST ROOM
from dark and dingy to moody guest retreat

Once the darkest corner of the house, now afternoon light filters in, and pale blue feels right at home.

BEFORE
Dark and oppressive, the front room was the simplest makeover, yet the one I worried about most, due to the lack of light.

AFTER
An exercise in trusting your instincts, this room now feels right at home enveloped in cottage wallpaper.

"Sometimes the rooms you worry about the most become the ones you sneak away to with a book."

Guest Bedroom
MOOD BOARD

dark vintage style wallpaper

COLOURS

floral and gingham mix textiles

repurposed furniture

cream chimney breast

cosy and restful

accents and decor

the guest bedroom

Other than the bathroom, the front room was the gloomiest corner of the cottage. Used as the bedroom for its deceased owner, it was the room where daylight barely dared enter. During our initial inspection, I worried that no amount of renovation would ever bring in enough light to make this room feel inviting. Some suggested embracing the darkness and leaning into a moodier aesthetic, and while I love a dramatic space, my goal for Blackbird Cottage was to prove that old homes don't have to be dim and dreary. I didn't want to turn on a lamp just to dust the mantel.

The transformation happened over the course of a week. Once the plasterers finished sheeting and sanding, the room felt immediately refreshed, but it was the first coats of primer that worked real magic. Suddenly, light bounced around in a way it never had. Replacing the verandah roof and adding clear Laserlight panels above the exterior of the windows allowed natural light to flood the room, turning it from a shadowy den into a space filled with possibility.

For the guest room, I wanted a distinctly cottage-style feel, but nothing too feminine or frilly. Since the room doesn't have a permanent occupant (though it's where our son and his partner stay when they visit), I aimed for something timeless, balanced, and welcoming.

The wallpaper, a deep green floral by Boråstapeter, was the perfect choice. Inspired by 1920s patterns, it nods to vintage without feeling dated, and despite being a floral, it doesn't make the room feel fussy or girly.

wrapped in wallpaper and trimmed in green

At first, I hesitated to wrap the room in the print, worried it might absorb too much light. So I did something I never do: I tried a feature wall behind the bed. And I regretted it for the year it stayed that way. After twelve months of living with it, I knew, emphatically, that feature wall wasn't right for this house. The rest of the walls must be papered. A couple of days (and plenty of ladder climbing) later, the room felt transformed. I'd enveloped it in the best way. Now it was cosy, restful, and full of character.

To keep the look cohesive, I carried the green trim from the hallway into the guest room, painting the window frame and doorway. Against the wallpaper, it adds beautiful depth, while the cream-painted ceiling and chimney breast keep the room feeling light, bouncing daylight from the opposite window throughout the space. The mantel, also finished in green, grounds the room. A vintage mirror, originally earmarked for the bathroom, hangs beside it. The frame, once a dull brown, came alive with a little gold Rub'n'Buff. On the wall, a wreath made from apple branches and tied with a soft green ribbon adds a handmade touch. It's the kind of detail that makes a cottage room feel special.

The room's lighting was another key decision. Because it had previously felt dark, I needed to think carefully about how the space would function in all conditions. The rattan pendant light casts a soft, diffused glow that pairs beautifully with the delicate wall sconces, offering guests a cosy reading light in the evenings. Thanks to rechargeable globes, I didn't need to wire the sconces in. The lights can be removed if my style changes. I simply charge the globes before guests arrive and leave the remotes by the bedside table.

The armoire, once painted black during its days at the farm, was carefully stripped back to reveal the natural grain and carved details of the timber. Rather than reinstall solid doors, I added vintage-inspired floral fabric panels—echoing the wallpaper, but with enough variation to hold interest. The twisted columns and ornate carving make it a statement piece, while the softened panels enhance its cottage charm.

The fabric for the gathered panels on this little wardrobe was purchased years ago, but never used until now. Sometimes, it takes a while to find a home that's just right for certain things. That's the joy of a curated collection

LAYERED BEDROOM TEXTURES
a simple checklist for seasonal living

A well-layered bedroom feels collected, not styled, like an invitation to unwind. These are the elements I return to again and again: natural fibres, soft pattern, and thoughtful texture. Together, they create that effortless cosiness that makes a bedroom feel truly lived in.

FOR THE BED
- Linen sheets for a relaxed look
- Cotton percale or flannelette sheets for colder months
- Two quilts in complementary patterns or textures
- A coverlet or light blanket
- A wool blanket or vintage eiderdown
- Frayed-edge or ruffled pillowcases
- Feather cushions in florals, gingham, and ticking stripes
- A bed skirt or valance to hide under bed storage

WINDOW DRESSINGS
- Linen curtain panels or soft stripes
- Block-printed fabric
- Rattan Roman blinds

EXTRAS TO ELEVATE
- A handmade or vintage-style lamp
- Patchwork throws
- Monogrammed pillows
- A basket of folded throws
- A bedroom chair

UNDERFOOT + AROUND THE ROOM
- A Persian-style rug
- Chunky jute or flatweave kilim
- Sheepskin or wool mats
- Patterned fabric-wrapped storage boxes under the bed

A ROOM OF ONE'S OWN
from drab beginnings to a storybook space

The door lock was installed upside down, so we decided to leave it. A little charm, a lot of character.

BEFORE  AFTER

Once a parlour, light flooded the front room. A dark floor border hinted at where Victorian rugs once lay.

Now a storybook retreat, it's the perfect workspace and guest room. Fresh paint and green wallpaper gave it life.

 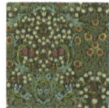

"I didn't choose any of these wallpapers, but they led me to the pattern that felt just right."

Office + Bedroom
MOOD BOARD

antique writer's ephemira

COLOURS

Vintage desk

soft green hues

walnut book storage

Jane Austen Inspired

A ROOM FOR A BIBLIOPHILE
Once a parlour, now an office, bedroom & creation space

A DESK THAT'S SEEN MANY VIEWS | NOW HAS A VIEW FROM MY OFFICE

Working from home, for myself, was something I dreamed of for years. But while we were raising a family and juggling a mortgage, the stability of teaching, complete with school holidays, was more a sensible choice. Creativity, though, has always been at the core of who I am. Whether I'm writing, making something with my hands, or decorating our home, I feel most like myself when I'm creating.

As a girl, I had dance lessons, spending weekends competing in eisteddfods. Later, I learned pottery and taught myself guitar. When I became a wife and mother, sewing, embroidery and DIY became creative outlets that often saved us money, too. That frugal mindset hasn't changed. I still believe if I can do something myself, and make it look professional, I should give it a try. That said, there are jobs I know better than to attempt. I have no desire for our walls to crumble or for visitors to comment on my handiwork as they back out the front door. With all that in mind, the opportunity to create a dedicated workspace of my own was exciting.

And I make no apologies for the fact that this room is decidedly feminine. Even if I'm not that girlie a girl.

In our previous homes, I carved out office nooks wherever I could—on the dining table, in the family room, even squeezed into a corner of the bedroom. But the spots I gravitated toward were always by a window. At the Glasshouse, I had a dedicated office near the front door where I could watch sheep graze as I worked. I used that space every single day. At the farm, though, my office was in the attic. Was it pretty? Absolutely. Functional? Yes. Did I ever actually use it? Not once. Apparently, a window view is non-negotiable.

a space for creativity

My office here at Blackbird Cottage overlooks the street too, with a double aspect that keeps it filled with natural light all day. I've tested both windows, but the spot where I now sit, shaded by the verandah, looking out to the box hedge Gavin planted, is the winner.

Originally, this room was likely a parlour or dining room. The name of one inhabitant who slept here is engraved into the window pane. At some point, the fireplace was removed and the chimney boarded over to block the draughts. We've seen this done in plenty of old homes and, without fail, we always reverse it. It's easy enough to stuff the chimney with insulation and regain the look of an open fireplace, minus the icy wind.

The bones of the room told a clear story. Hand-routed ceiling battens hinted at someone's attempt to elevate the cottage beyond its humble beginnings. The doorway was framed in the sweetest black wallpaper border—swagged flowers that looked like the embroidery on an old pair of braces. A pale blue colonial-style wallpaper once wrapped the room, and the floorboards had been stained around the edges to give the illusion of a full dark floor. It was clearly once a proud, pretty room, and I wanted to return it to that. Of all the spaces in the house, this one feels the most authentic to its era.

LITTLE KEEPSAKE No 14
This tattered swatch was uncovered near the bedroom chimney. It's a fragment of someone else's idea of home. One day, I'll use the pattern to start something new.

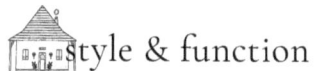 style & function

Because the office needs to do so much: writing, tutoring, creating, exercising, and even hosting overnight guests, the decor had to be both functional and flexible. When our daughter visits from abroad, it transforms into her bedroom, and since I store her book collection here, she's dubbed it the 'library room.' For this reason, the furniture choices needed to be flexible and light, or in the case of her bed, easy to dismantle and store.

The starting point for the scheme was wallpaper. I sampled dozens of prints, but when I pinned the fresh green and cream Morris & Co. pattern to the wall, I knew. It was perfect. Even better, the original print dates to 1883, just a few years after the cottage was likely built. Its climbing vines and stylised flowers feel like they're pulling the outdoors in and the cream was, coincidentally, a perfect match for the paint colour I selected for the ceiling and rest of the house. I didn't hesitate. Despite the cost, I wallpapered all four walls, having learned that valuable lesson in the sister room across the hall. (aka, the guest room.) The result is a calming room that feels warm and light all year round.

furnishings with a past

The remainder of the furniture is intentionally simple. A vintage desk with cabriole legs sits beneath the window, its single drawer stocked with glue sticks and the bulldog clips I cannot live without. The desk was an antique shop find some ten years ago, and has been with me in each home since. The paint colour has altered, depending on the room the desk is in, but the function it performs has not.

I decorate the top of the desk and windowsill behind seasonally. A nest in spring, shells in summer, a tiny tree at Christmas. Sometimes it's an autumn branch from the garden. This is a small ritual that keeps me inspired. An armchair that has no other home waits to be recovered in the corner, and an old leather trunk stores blankets and pillows for the bed. Storage is essential in a room like this. My old pine bookcase, which Gavin once suggested we get rid of, fits snugly beside the chimney. It's housed everything from picture books to tax files over the years, and now it holds stationery and supplies in its raw state.

On the other side of the chimney, a small walnut secretaire stores craft materials and our daughter's book collection. Both pieces stay put, but when guests are here, the desk is easily shifted to make room for a vintage double bed and cosy bedding.

The wallpaper is the star of the room, so I've kept the artwork minimal. Beside the window hang two watercolours painted over a century ago by my great-great-aunts. A framed print titled, *Boundless in Bloom* by Vietnamese-born painter Duy Huynh, sits above the chimney. It brings a whimsical quality that I love to the room. Near the door, an auction find depicting a country house we once hoped to buy makes me smile. Its watery tones and timber

a vintage office chair that may have seen better days

frame echo the wallpaper and keep the palette consistent. There's a photo of our children in their teenage years, a porcelain doll from my grandmother, and a small wire heart I bought on a trip with a friend. These small sentimental items make the room feel like it's mine, right down to the button from my daughter that says, "Cheer Mum," stabbed into the frill of the lamp.

A rose-hued vintage rug anchors the room with just the right amount of colour. I can't say I'm a fan of the washable rug for this home. They're a little thin underfoot for a cold climate. But with the addition of a thick felt underlay, it feels right here.

COLLECTED & USEFUL
office things I love

A home office should feel personal, not corporate, so I collect things that embody that idea. Below are the objects that help me stay organised, feel inspired, and keep the space looking like part of the cottage, not a tech hub. Pretty, practical, and a little bit personal.

FOR THE DESK
- A sweet desk (mine was bought when we moved back to Tasmania)
- A comfortable office chair
- Vessels for pens
- A supply of good stationery + pens
- Notebook or journal
- Small seasonal decor

AT THE WINDOW
- Bottles or jars
- A light-filtering curtain
- A comfortable view
- A chair nearby for when you need a new perspective

TUCKED AWAY
- Rattan baskets, document holders and boxes
- Hidden storage: drawers, desk, chest of drawers
- Vintage baskets for larger documents
- A cabinet with doors and drawers
- Lidded boxes or tins

TO INSPIRE
- Books, both vintage and new
- A personal memento
- A vision board or pinboard
- Postcards, photos, or quotes tucked into frames

A bookcase might be for storage but it's also an opportunity for showing off collectables against a backdrop of books and boxes

A WASHROOM WITH CHARACTER
from tired tub to beautiful utility room

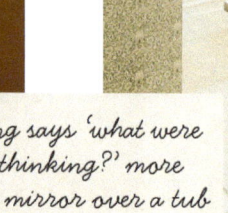

Nothing says 'what were they thinking?' more than a mirror over a tub or carpet in a bathroom.

BEFORE

The bathroom was the fossil of the house. Forgotten and dated with carpeted floors and a boxed-in tub, it showed its age.

AFTER

Now airy and practical, it pairs utility and charm with the help of cottage-style accents.

"A small footprint isn't a limitation. It's an invitation to be creative, to achieve the look you want within your budget."

Bathroom/Laundry
MOOD BOARD

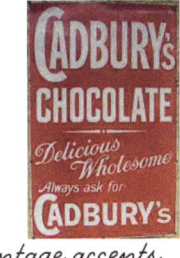

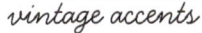
vintage accents

COLOURS

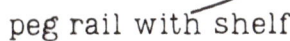
peg rail with shelf

hidden laundry

shower feature wall

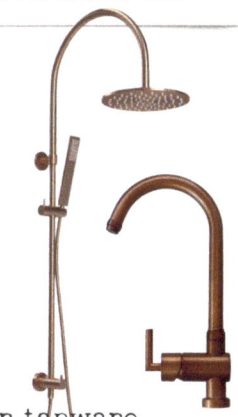

heritage feel in soft green

copper tapware

THE SMALLEST ROOM
A room thats both practical and poetic

A VANITY CLEVERLY HIDES
OTHER TASKS |
MULTIFUNCTIONAL SPACES

For many years, we treated the bathroom as a secondary space. It was important for its function, but rarely a design priority. If it was presentable, that was enough. With tight budgets and a busy family, renovating a bathroom always felt like a luxury. And like the bedroom in past renovations, we simply left the bathroom till last.

I often think of the one in the Dollhouse. It had a beautiful original terrazzo floor in the palest yellow. The avocado fittings made me shudder, but the layout was practical, and the room was generous enough for a large family. We always meant to renovate. We wanted to rejuvenate the floor, replace the tapware and spray the tub and basin. But life changed, we moved to WA, and the house was sold before we had the chance. I still wonder whether the owners modernised it. Maybe they saw its charm like I did, and chose a sympathetic restoration. Or maybe they did nothing at all.

Since living in that house, our approach to bathrooms has changed. If the budget allows, we prioritise updating, knowing the improvements will lift both daily life and long-term value. At Blackbird Cottage we had the opportunity to start from scratch yet our aim was simple: create a bathroom that did the hard work, but one that felt as considered and characterful as every other room in the house. It was, after all, the smallest room with the biggest job.

a multi-tasking layout

The bathroom at Blackbird Cottage might be the smallest room in the house, but it does a lot of heavy lifting. It's our only bathroom, and also functions as our laundry. Sandwiched between the kitchen and lounge, and seen from the back entry. . . Let's just say I wanted a wow moment as you opened the door and stepped inside.

When we bought the cottage, the bathroom and laundry were separate rooms. The laundry stretched along the back of the house, prime real estate we wanted to reclaim for the kitchen. The bathroom, while larger than expected for a home of this age, hadn't been touched in decades. It was so dark and grimy I refused to go in there. I shut the door and waited for the day it could be demolished.

Council restrictions meant we couldn't move the bathroom, and space was limited in the kitchen area. So we reimagined the functions of the space, trying to allow for two people to use the room at the same time and give each of them privacy. After many iterations, we created a compact, multifunctional space and expanded the kitchen and dining areas in the process. To do this, we shifted the bathroom door from the centre of the wall to one side. This gave us room to install the oven on the other side of the wall and, inside the bathroom, make a cubicle for the toilet.

We created a vanity moment as you enter the bathroom, tucking it inside the door and putting a full height wall behind it. This hides the toilet, acheiving our goal of two people being in the room together. With the shower hidden behind a second feature wall, privacy is maintained at all times.

Likewise, the washer-dryer, cleaning supplies and brooms are hidden behind double doors, disguised as part of the cabinetry. Deep shelves inside provide generous storage without adding visual weight, and there's plenty of room for linen, bags and anything else we need to hide.

As a bonus, the 'laundry tub' required by council became an opportunity for a second vanity area. This was achieved by swapping a traditional look sink for a deep, circular porcelain sink and adding copper tapware, a reclaimed timber shelf and extra wallpaper to echo the shower wall. Handwashing can be done when needed, but with the addition of a shaving mirror we now have a light filled area for putting on makeup or shaving.

DIY details

As with every room in the cottage, we layered in personality after the initial build was complete. Gavin built a peg rail to match the back-door version, and I repurposed copper tubing as a curtain rod. It's an inexpensive, vintage-inspired detail also seen in the dining nook. We added thin trim to the laundry cupboard doors to give them a more traditional profile, and I used leftover wallpaper from the office, sealed behind plexiglass, as a splashback above the laundry sink. These are the small, resourceful touches that elevate the space without overextending the budget.

The mirror was a sale find and a perfect size for the wall above the vanity. Its floral details softened the tile, and a coat of custom copper spray paint warmed the palette of the room. That copper tone ties in with the brushed tapware from ABI Interiors, which we used at the laundry sink, bathroom vanity, and in the shower.

I've never loved store-bought vanity units. While practical, they're often too modern in style for the look I love. The quality, as with kitchen cabinetry, doesn't always justify the cost in my book, so my preferred option is a converted piece. For this bathroom, I used a 1940's oak dressing table without the mirrored top. I sanded the varnish off and applied a lime stain-varnish to lighten the tone. Porcelain knobs with antique brass centres replaced the broken pulls and marble-look Mirastone was placed on top to create a waterproof surface for the fluted ceramic basin. The cabriole legs soften the hard edges of the bathroom and continue the collected feel used throughout the house.

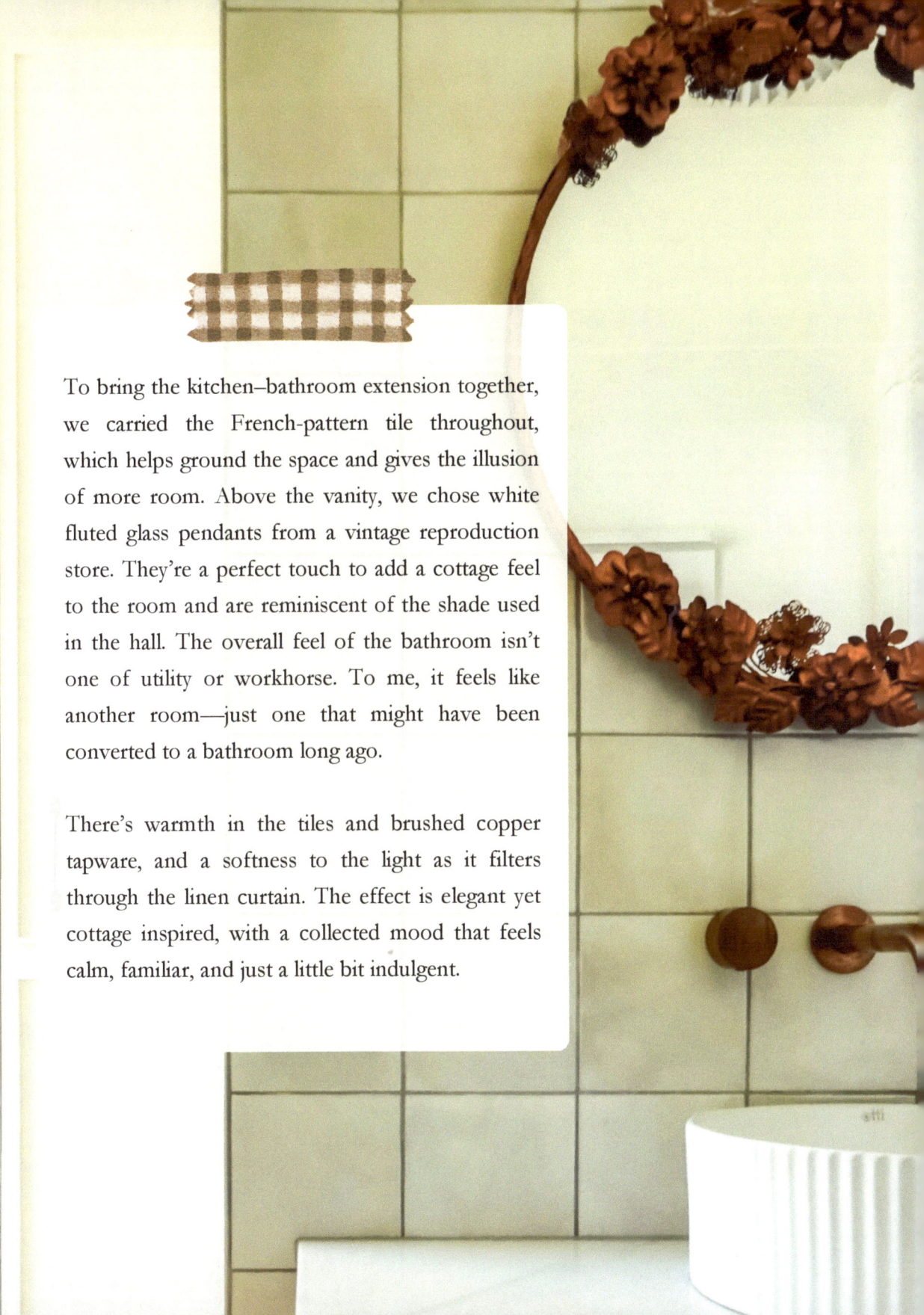

To bring the kitchen–bathroom extension together, we carried the French-pattern tile throughout, which helps ground the space and gives the illusion of more room. Above the vanity, we chose white fluted glass pendants from a vintage reproduction store. They're a perfect touch to add a cottage feel to the room and are reminiscent of the shade used in the hall. The overall feel of the bathroom isn't one of utility or workhorse. To me, it feels like another room—just one that might have been converted to a bathroom long ago.

There's warmth in the tiles and brushed copper tapware, and a softness to the light as it filters through the linen curtain. The effect is elegant yet cottage inspired, with a collected mood that feels calm, familiar, and just a little bit indulgent.

WHERE THE GARDEN GROWS

A made from scratch space, designed for beauty and utility

FIELD NOTES No 6

Photographed January 2024

ROUGH-SAWN STAKES AS
CHICKEN BARRIER | BACK YARD

A simple barrier of stakes mark the line between order and chaos, apples and gladioli on one side, hens and puppies on the other. No frills, just function, and plenty of charm.

A GARDEN FROM SCRATCH
from bare patch to multifunctional outdoor space

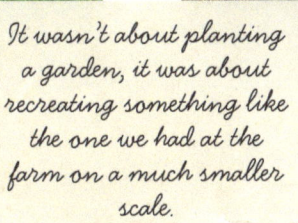

It wasn't about planting a garden, it was about recreating something like the one we had at the farm on a much smaller scale.

BEFORE

A basic lawn with trees that no longer bore fruit and an aluminium shed that had seen better days

AFTER

Now open and layered with hedges, natives and cottage planting, it's a place to gather, potter, and relax.

"A traditional garden, designed to thrive without fuss. Beauty, made simple."

THE GARDEN THAT GROWS

A made from scratch space, designed for beauty, utility and a little wonder

In 2023, Blackbird Cottage had no garden to speak of, just a scattering of overgrown fruit trees and a tall metal fence that shut out the view. It was a typical suburban block, pointing back to a time when garden aesthetics weren't important and outdoor entertaining didn't really happen. I could imagine the washing hanging on the clothesline, and the odd game of backyard cricket, but it wasn't a space to spend time, so we knew from the outset that formulating a design and planting out had to start straight away. Rescued cuttings and sentimental favourites from the cut flower garden at the farm waited patiently in their pots, needing permanent homes. And gardens, like friendships, take time to grow.

Gavin loves gardening which meant that, somewhere along the way, an unspoken rule emerged: he designs the outside, and I look after the inside. Naturally then, he took the lead in shaping the exterior around the cottage. I offered input, but the structure is all his.

The first change came when we removed the back fence. It was a simple but transformative alteration that gave us a bay view, one that changes with the time of day and season. To preserve that openness, he planted a Pittosporum hedge, kept just above waist height, then added a metal gate to open directly onto the banks of the rivulet. Inside the hedge, a stretch of hidden chicken wire keeps Bonnie and Winnie safe (and out of the water). Our hens, who came with us from the farm, peck happily on the banks of the creek before returning to their coop each evening.

Rather than divide the space with harsh lines, Gavin continued the hedging theme, this time with mauve-flowering Westringia to define each garden zone. Old trees were removed, the land gently levelled, and a circular lawn laid out to soften the square edges and give us somewhere to sit on warm days. Around it, he dug cottage-style borders to fill with our favourite perennials, bulbs, and annuals. We set aside a generous portion of the budget to plant mature trees so the garden would feel established from the start. Over time, the beds will spill onto the grass, blurring the line between formal and informal.

making an impression

Early photos of Blackbird Cottage from the 1900s showed a white picket fence, and, in the early iterations of our design, we were convinced we'd reinstate it. But when we saw the house with its modern panel fencing gone, the light and openness changed our minds. A low box hedge would soften the facade, dampen road noise, and lend a more relaxed, cottagey feel. It also let the character of the house shine, rather than hiding it away. From that decision, the rest of the outdoor spaces followed.

On one side of the house, we set out a pair of symmetrical garden beds retained with low brick edging that made way for a gravel path between.

Colourbond fencing: the first thing to go

English Box hedge to soften the concrete footpath outside

Each bed centres on a mature crabapple tree for year-round shape, privacy, and a spring burst of blossom. Beneath them, seasonal bulbs in white and yellow bring a cheerful show for both us and passing walkers.

Sandstone gravel skirts the base of the cottage, visually separating it from the garden beds and linking the paths around the house. The low box hedge carries across the front boundary, guiding the eye without closing anything off. It will grow to the height of the new heritage-style front gate. Near the street, we tucked in a small gravel bay for guest parking that looks planned, not improvised. And to complete the picture, driveway gates that mirror the front entrance create a sense of arrival. It's structured, but still welcoming.

the kitchen garden gate

Though far smaller than our farm garden, the kitchen garden had to fulfil the same purpose: fresh fruit and vegetables year-round. Downsizing meant we had to be more deliberate, planning for practicality, ease of maintenance, and beauty in equal measure.

To separate the front yard from the north-east side where this garden would be, we built an entry into the back yard composed of a side fence, arbor, and gate between the crabapple trees. The fence is a mesh structure, covered by native Maidenhair Creeper. It grows vigorously but is easily trimmed to create a hedge effect along the fence and over the arbor. This evergreen climber's tight habit creates privacy, security and a sense of arrival.

Inside the gate, Gavin designed raised garden beds to echo the style of Huon Valley apple crates. Built at hip height and from the same timber as the shed, they visually tie the far corners of the garden together. The beds are deep, so they were filled with branches and garden rubble to begin, then topped with fertiliser, topsoil and mulch. As the soil compacts, more is added. Along the paths, pots, espaliered fruit, and vertical frames hold our favourite herbs and berries. These give the productive side of the garden a sense of formality, as well as year-round structure.

a henhouse fit for queens

On one side sits the timber-framed henhouse, its roof covered in salvaged tin from the cottage. The walls are mesh panels, now hidden beneath thornless blackberries and grapevines. These climbers not only soften the structure but provide shade and extra foraging for the hens. At ground level, small herb boxes give them something fresh to nibble on. Our girls, led by Dorothy, love to peck on these when they're indoors.

a new side fence to the kitchen garden

A worm farm turns kitchen scraps into nutrient-rich compost, and the chicken litter and bedding are worked back into the vegetable beds and garden. Beneath the potting table, tools and equipment are kept close at hand, ready for the next planting. The productive section continues through a second arch, threaded with jasmine. Beyond it, rows of raspberries, blackberries, and elderflower trees create a living privacy screen. A layer of native plantings, featuring Bottlebrush and Waratah, becomes a source for rustic bouquets in the house. In summer and autumn, these rows reward us with baskets of fruit, while underneath, a drift of Chilean guava, brought with us from the farm, blooms happily. Its berries are a favourite of the hens and a sweet garnish for autumn drinks.

"The garden hums with new beginnings: blossoms reaching toward the sun, fruit heavy on the branch and hens at the gate."

CREATE A GARDEN THAT SINGS
filled with wildlife and produce

the garden entry

Little rustic birds perch on the front fence, marking the way into the kitchen garden.

kitchen produce

Timber planters brimming with vegetables keep the garden both orderly and abundant.

lawn visitors

Wattle birds, galahs, and fairy wrens flit between blooms, bringing the garden to life.

cottage planting

Daisies, lavender, and cottage blooms tumble together in an easy blend of colour.

espalier spacesaver

Pears ripen along neat wires, their fruit framed by leaves and sun.

THE COTTAGE MADE BY HAND

Simple crafts and projects to bring beauty into the home

FIELD NOTES *No 7*

Baked Dec 23 2024

GINGERBREAD BISCUITS | FAMILY TRADITION WITH ICED DETAILS | MAKERS: EVERYONE

The kitchen turned into a scatter of flour, icing, and laughter. Each biscuit was given too many sprinkles, far too much pink icing, and enough love to make them disappear by the next morning.

THE COTTAGE MADE BY HAND

Simple crafts and projects to bring beauty into the home

I've always found a satisfaction in making things by hand. Long before I owned a home or even had the thought of owning one, I was at the kitchen table with scraps of fabric and my grandmother beside me. She taught me to sew, to make do, to treasure the work of turning nothing into something. There were days, as a young woman, I'd arrive at her house wanting a new dress to wear out that night. We'd rummage through her stash of fabric and patterns and she'd pull a piece from this, and one from that, to create the look I wanted. Then, I'd sew it together and an original outfit would be born. We spent hours painting on fabric and sewing sequins on my costumes for dancing competitions.

Those early days left their imprint. It was never about perfection. It was about care, intention, and the deep satisfaction of crafting something with your own hands. It was about the joy of creating and the handing down of traditions and lessons from another time.

Not every project needs to be grand or time-consuming. Life is not always about a huge renovation. Sometimes, the most rewarding moments come from quick, hands-on tasks that offer a sense of completion in an afternoon. There's a joy in watching something take shape under your fingers like a lampshade transformed, a tablecloth hemmed, or a wreath formed from foraged twigs. These small wins build confidence and beauty in equal measure.

This chapter is filled with simple, comforting projects that invite you to slow down, create beauty, and make your home more deeply your own. Each piece, like each memory, will be a thing of beauty stitched into the shape of a life lived with heart, and a home created with your own hands.

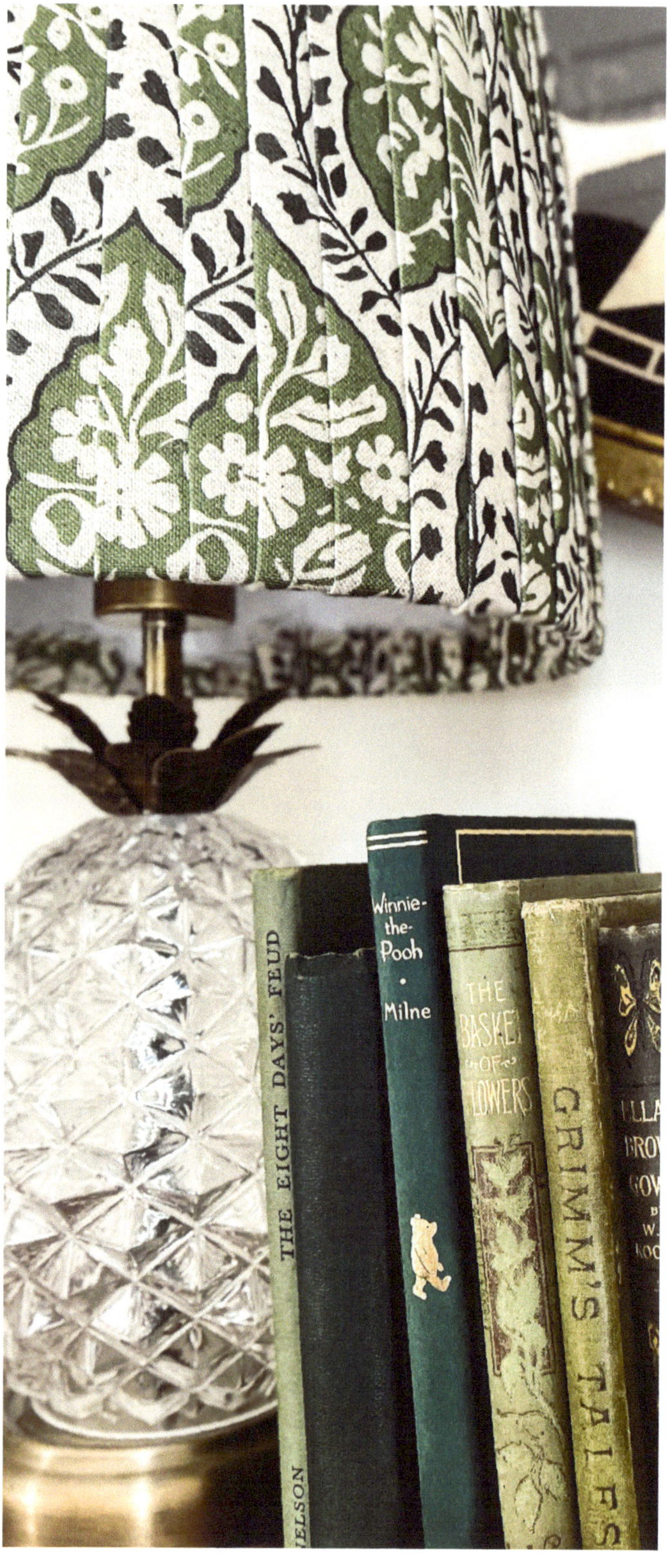
THE EIGHT DAYS' FEUD
Winnie-the-Pooh
Milne

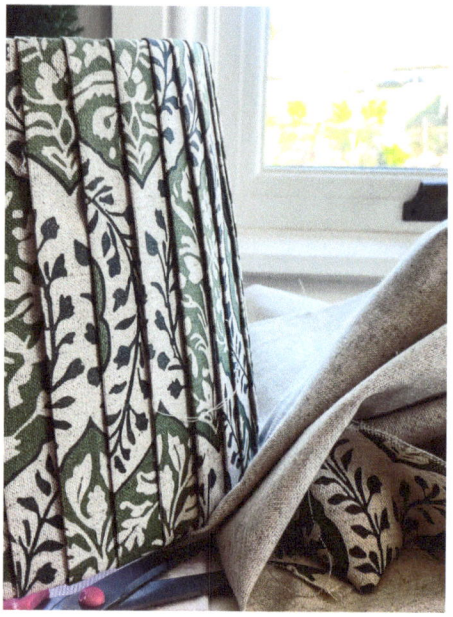

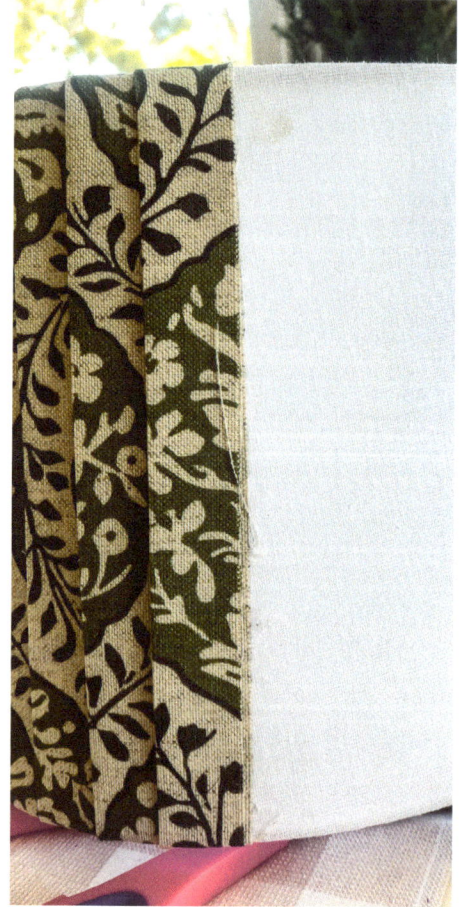

A PLEATED LAMPSHADE
a project for a corner of the home

Sometimes, the smallest transformations bring the most delight. When the shade on my favourite pineapple lamp finally gave way to wear and time, I could have tossed it aside and bought something new. But instead, I took it as an invitation to try a craft I'd seen online, make something by hand, and to bring a little more softness into the room.

you will need:
- A plain lampshade
- About a metre of lightweight fabric (cotton or linen is ideal)
- Fabric glue or a hot glue gun
- Scissors or a rotary cutter
- Measuring tape
- Optional: ribbon or bias tape for finishing, Scotchguard fabric spray

to make:
- Choose a lightweight fabric in a soft, room-friendly print—something that lets the light glow through. I used a leafy green block print that felt right among the textures of our home.
- Measure the height of your lampshade and cut narrow strips a little longer—around 4cm wide. Fold each strip lengthwise and press to create gentle pleats.
- Starting at the back seam, glue each strip along the top and bottom edges of the shade. Fold the extra fabric over the rim and secure it inside, spacing pleats evenly as you go.
- For the final strip, tuck in the raw edges before gluing. Trim any loose threads and, if desired, finish the inner edge with ribbon or bias tape.
- A mist of Scotchgard can protect the fabric, though I prefer the worn-in beauty of untreated cloth.

AIR DRY CLAY DIFFUSER DISCS
A delicate, scented project for gifting or hanging

This project began with a leftover batch of air dry clay from Christmas, a simple material with endless possibility. I intended to make something entirely different, but when that didn't go to plan, I turned instead to something sweeter: little hanging diffuser discs. These pieces make beautiful gifts and can be tucked into drawers, wardrobes, or corners that need a touch of scent. Mine currently hangs off the knob of the kitchen dresser.

you will need:

- Air dry clay
- A rolling pin
- cookie cutter
- straw or skewer
- Dried flowers, leaves, lace, or an embossed rolling pin
- A wire rack (for drying)
- Fine sandpaper
- Gold paint and a fine brush (or a metallic marker)
- String or twine
- Essential oil of your choice
- *Optional*: matte varnish for the front

to make:

- Knead air-dry clay until soft, then roll it out to about 3mm thick. For even pressure, roll between two timber guides.
- Press in texture with lace, a leaf, or a patterned roller, then cut discs with a cookie cutter. Use a skewer or straw to poke a hole near the top.
- Smooth edges with a damp finger and dry on a rack for 24 hours. Once dry, sand lightly. You can highlight the texture with gold paint and seal the front with matte varnish (leave the back unsealed for oil).
- Thread with string or leather, add a few drops of essential oil to the back, and hang in a wardrobe, near your desk, or anywhere that needs a little lift.

ABOUT THE AUTHOR

"Home isn't built in a day. But it helps if you've lived in eleven of them, written about love and darkness, and know how to boss a bookshelf."

Lindy Rahn is a writer, renovator, decorator and teacher who's lived in eleven homes, yet still chases the dream of a sandstone cottage. The author of romantic comedies and gritty love stories, she turned her hand to sharing her signature decorating style on Instagram in 2018, where she's nurtured a community of loyal followers.

A self taught decorator, Lindy was raised on the idea that making it yourself is as good a solution as any when you have no money.

Her approach to decorating and life is unapologetically practical, a little sentimental, and stubbornly curated. If it's floral, gilded or able to be repurposed, it probably has a place in her house.

Lindy lives with her husband, Gavin, and their two dogs, Bonnie and Winnie, at Blackbird Cottage—a characterful 1870s home in Tasmania's Huon Valley. When she's not busy shaping her cottage, you'll find her walking the dogs, enjoying a treat at the local bakery, or sharing cocktails with friends.

THANK YOU

To everyone who's followed the journey, sent kind words, or simply nodded along while flipping pages—thank you. This book began with an old cottage and a head full of ideas, but it came to life because of the people who helped hold the ladder (sometimes literally) during the renovation process: TradCo Architectural Hardware, Wallpaper Direct, Tint Paint, The Drillhall Emporium, Fat Shack Vintage, and the small businesses who contributed to the decor.

A special acknowledgement to Maddy and the team at TradCo for asking me to be part of their advertising and allowing me to use their images of the cottage. Also, to Eliska Sharp for the stunning photography and *Country Style Magazine* for allowing me to reprint our kitchen and portrait shots.

To the readers who've embraced crooked walls, gingham everything, and stories that ramble as much as I do, you are my people. Thank you for sharing the joy of a magazine feature and the pain of leaving our farm and losing our beloved pooch, Poppy.

Thank you for the little unexpected gifts in the mail I never asked for, the surprise meetings in the supermarket and drive-bys of our house. They were awkward, but they demonstrate your appreciation for this house and our hard work.

Thank you for the laughter, encouragement, and enthusiastic support of my most hare-brained ideas. (Especially when I post polls, then don't follow your advice.)

And to Gavin, chief builder, problem-solver, idea-wrangler, and the one who never once questioned why I was hanging wallpaper inside a cabinet, this cottage would still be a tin-roofed daydream without you.

With love and gratitude,

Lindy xoxo

www.ingramcontent.com/pod-product-compliance
Lightning Source LLC
Chambersburg PA
CBHW041507220426
43661CB00017B/1274